From Madras to Chennai

and some of life in between

Fran Forsyth

2QT Publishing

First Edition published 2025 by

2QT Publishing

Copyright © Fran Forsyth
The right of Fran Forsyth to be identified as the author of this work has been asserted by her in accordance with the Copyright, Designs and Patents Act 1988

All rights reserved. This book is for personal use only: no part of this book is to be sold, reproduced, in any shape or form, or by way of trade, stored in a retrieval system or transmitted in any form or by any means, electronic, mechanical, photocopying, recording, be lent, re-sold, hired out or otherwise circulated in any form of binding or cover without prior permission of the copyright holder.

Publisher Disclaimer:
The events in this memoir are described according to the Author's recollection; recognition and understanding of the events and individuals mentioned and are in no way intended to mislead or offend. As such the Publisher does not hold any responsibility for any inaccuracies or opinions expressed by the author.

Cover Image ©: 'Ayah' by Liz Hutchinson
Instagram page: elizabethhutchinsonart

Printed in UK by IngramSpark

A CIP catalogue record for this book is available
from the British Library

ISBN 978-1-9193271-0-5

Dedication

This book is for Molly, Basil and Jan.
And for Annimmal. With love.

Thanks

Thank you to those who have encouraged me to get this far with my book – for your time, your interest and enthusiasm, and for your thoughtful words. I am truly grateful. Thank you Liz Hutchinson for letting me use your painting – 'Ayah' – which is so perfect for this book. And thank you to Patrick for your love, patience and care and for sharing India memories – my old ones and our new.

Contents

Dedication	iii
Thanks	v
Foreword	1
PART ONE - The beginning - In India	
Ayah	5
Khader Nawaz Khan Road	10
The Club	22
School and Mrs de Silva	30
The Afternoon at Mette's House	35
A Picnic at Sadras	39
Lady Bountiful	48
A Sailor is Just for Christmas	51
How We Got to Kodai	58
Kodai Life	65
Leaving	75
Becoming number 60	77
A Weekend Out	85
Riverview	89
PART TWO - The Messy Middle	
Decisions	103
The Trip	108

Back to England	113
Yorkshire	117
Mum and Jan	120
PART THREE - The End	
India, 2002	139
Staying in Cuddalore	148
Room 2	154
Back to Yorkshire	160
India, 2003	163
Finally	172

Foreword

India is my 'go to' place. It is where I go in my mind when I want the comfort of familiar images or when I can't sleep and need to remember there are other perspectives and a parallel universe thousands of miles from mine. It is also where I actually go by plane, with a visa and plans and Imodium in my luggage. I lived there until I was eight years old and it has punctuated my life ever since. It has been a buffer zone, a place to take stock or to build up the strength to make changes. It is where I feel happy and at home and strongly connected to people from my past.

This book begins in India and, after the muddle of middle life, comes full circle back to India where the end begins. It is about the progress of life and some of the places, people and happenings which have had an impact on me. It is about my family: my mum and dad, Molly and Basil; and my sister, Jan.

I started this book with the wish to produce a record and mark of my existence, for myself and for a few people close to me. Increasingly now I feel that the places and people I write of deserve to exist in the light of day instead of inside my head. In some small way perhaps I can give them posterity. How lovely, and right, that someone else may think of Jan and for my ayah to be known by someone other than me. And if this writing can evoke some images, memories or meaning for even a few other people, I would be pleased beyond words.

When writing about India I am writing about my own experiences of that country. I am not attempting to describe or comment on the history, politics or other significant aspects of the country itself. I feel it's important to say that I am absolutely not oblivious to those aspects, but they are not what this book is about.

May 2025

Part One:
The Beginning – In India

Ayah

I was eight years old when wooden boxes with metal edges suddenly arrived in our house. In the hot afternoons on the upstairs veranda, under a fan, my mum talked to me about England. She wanted me to know where I was going to live. She told me about the cool wet smell of gardens and the bright white sparkle of snow. About houses with carpets and steep sloping roofs and the feel of hot coal fires. She said you could drink fresh milk from a bottle and water straight from a tap. She thought all this would please me, but nothing she said could make me want to leave.

It was the early 1960s and we were living in India. British companies, like my dad's, had handed over to their new Indian owners and the process of transition was complete. My dad never fully left India. He returned for stints with his Indian colleagues right up to the year he died, and he would have been happy to die there. But foreign policy and economic goings-on all meant nothing to me. My only concern, more than friends or school or places, was how I would live without Ayah and how she would live without me.

Ayah's name was Annimmal but I just called her Ayah[1]. She wore tissue-light white saris which smelt of washing and sun. And there was a deeper smell of the coconut oil which she combed through her long grey hair. I would watch her hold flimsy metal pins between her lips as she stretched to fix her bun. The sleeves of her choli[2] cut into the tops of her arms, and the hooks and eyes at the front hung on by a thread which I expected to burst any minute. She was fleshy and soft to cuddle, which we were prone to do. There were large empty holes in her earlobes and in her nose a dark ruby stud in the shape of a tiny flower. When Ayah laughed, which she did very easily and often, her shoulders hunched and shook and she bowed her head as if she were shy and covered her mouth with her hand or the simple edge of her sari. She had two gold teeth at the back of her mouth which she used to let me look at. She said they were her insurance if she ever got really poor, and

---

1 *ayah*: in India, a nurse or maid.

2 *choli*: a short-sleeved top worn by Indian women.

I'd hug her tight, afraid of the thought that she'd ever need to use them.

These were our last afternoons. We walked hand in hand on scorching streets to some of her favourite places. She was Catholic and she liked the church the best. She covered her head with her sari and we dipped our fingers into the holy water and I'd copy her making the sign of the cross. "Do NOT swallow the water," she would whisper loudly; I was always tempted to taste it on my tongue. The church was large and pale inside with no glass in the high windows, so birds flew in to rest or nest behind the statues or the Stations of the Cross. The air was cooler than outside, shady and soft and full of the smell of melting candles and incense. Women knelt at the front of the church, their babies safe on the floor beside them wrapped in bundles of cloth. Their saris slipped from their heads and they lifted them over again and again, pulling the edge across their faces, covering their mouths while they murmured their prayers, in Tamil, over and over like a quiet background hum.

After Ayah's prayers we would visit the priest in his room at the back of the church. It always seemed dark and cluttered. He would welcome us and give each of us a small picture of Jesus, and sometimes Ayah would ask him to bless a new rosary. I walked away quietly, for a few moments, feeling subdued and holy.

Ayah also liked Gemini Film Studios. We'd wait for ages among the hot bright lights and thick make-up for one of the stars to appear and as soon as they did, she would become shy and giggling and make us walk away. Afterwards we'd sit in the shrivelled park nearby on spiky, prickling grass and ants the size of my toes. She would tell me the story and sing some songs from the film. She had a delicate voice and expressions in her eyes and she would wobble her head to the words.

Sometimes we sat on the speckled stone floor of the downstairs veranda, eating oranges and watching ants walk away with the peel. They appeared from the hole where the door bolt went down when we shut ourselves in for the night. I wondered what became of them then – if they were squashed or if they waited in a deeper tunnel until the bolt went up in the morning. While Ayah and I sat talking, or simply just being close, my mum would be busy somewhere else in the house and my sister, when she was home, would be listening to Cliff Richard or Elvis in her room. She had a pale-blue Decca record player and she endlessly played 'Blue Moon'.

This was where I lived and how I lived and who I lived with. My lucky life, which was about to change. And I was aware in some small way, and worried, about what this would mean to Ayah. The loss of her job, her home, our family, maybe her local friends.

Ayah wore two bangles I had given her as a present. If I went out without her I brought her something back, and when she went out on her days off she would bring me some small surprise wrapped up in the folds of her sari. She said I was five minutes good and ten minutes naughty and she knew I loved her more than the world and I knew that she loved me. She called me her sweet lime her sugar lump her petty cash her beauty face and she gave me lakhs[3] of kisses. I had spent nearly every day and every night since I was two with Ayah.

In those weeks of disruption the metal-edged boxes were filled and then sealed tight with wires. They were stamped and ready to collect. I roamed among them finding quiet corners where I could hide to think my thoughts and feel the dread of what this move would mean. It was my first great separation, a sort of footprint for some of those to come.

---

3 *lakh*: in India, a hundred thousand.

Khader Nawaz Khan Road

I first went to India when I was two, with my mum, my dad and my big sister Jan, who was nearly twelve years old. They had previously lived in Calcutta,[4] pre and post-Independence, and that is where I was conceived. I love it that I was conceived there. It makes me feel I have India in my bones and helps explain my feeling of an 'other-worldness' connection. Most people have their own 'India' I think – a place that's almost spookily familiar as if known from a previous life.

We went to Madras[5] on the south-east coast and we lived on Khader Nawaz Khan Road in Nungambakkam. Once you got the hang of it, those words were nice to say. They sound to me like the

---

4   now Kolkata.

5   Madras became Chennai in 1996. Throughout this book, I will use whichever name it had at the particular time I am referring to.

beginning of a children's poem. Khader Nawaz Khan Road Nungambakkam. That part of Chennai is now packed tight with buildings, mainly offices and upmarket shops. The roads appear to have changed direction and the house seems to face the wrong way. It was still there when I visited in January 2024. It was mucky and dilapidated with boards and wire fencing, wedged between buildings and traffic, thick pollution and noise. Despite the change, it was also still the same – the familiar symmetrical shape in Art Deco style with geometric lines along the outside and a sensible, easy layout. I knew all the rooms so well, where we had talked and slept and sat to eat together. Where we had lived our everyday lives.

I first revisited in 2002. The house was in reasonable condition then. The downstairs was being converted into a restaurant and the owner, who happened to be there when I arrived, was gracious and interested and allowed me to walk around.

In Jan's room I could picture her bed where she sometimes let me sit while she played her records and danced. I saw her dancing and the red and white dress she wore. Or she read to me from *Winnie the Pooh* with a wonderful rendition of Piglet; she made his voice sweet and squeaky. I loved the one about Pooh writing a hum for Piglet and how Piglet went pink when Pooh told him. He said there were seven verses in it. "'Seven?' said Piglet as carelessly as he could. 'You don't often get *seven* verses in a Hum, do you, Pooh?'" I still hear those books in Jan's voice, the tones she used for all the different characters.

My room was attached to hers and was really a dressing room, with a bathroom leading off. Jane the lizard lived behind a mirror on the bathroom wall. She was small and yellow and I could watch her come and go from my bed. I saw the back staircase where Ayah sat chatting to her friends, and the upstairs veranda where we all spent so much time. "Another drink?" my dad would ask. His was a G&T. And he'd probably talk about work, some imminent strike or developing the new Diamond Chain or a puja[6] at the factory. "Oh, that's interesting," my mum would say, wanting to know more about the puja. "Which god? How often? When?" She made notes of things she wanted to know and would look them up in the library. On the upstairs veranda I had my own small cane chair, pale yellow with red arms and there were glass-topped tables where the drinks and nibbles and ashtrays could go. In the evening the lamps were all turned on and a mist of tiny insects buzzed around them making a dreadful racket, with hollow thuds or sharp pings when larger moths or other winged creatures crashed into the bulbs. A

---

6 *puja*: a religious ceremony.

dark circle of dead bodies lay on the ground beneath them.

I wandered around the house and I could hear and see us as we had all been then. The clarity was overwhelming. And their absence. Dad, Jan and Mum, as large as life in my mind, were now dead. How could it be? All three of them? No other insider to our family life, to know how we had been when only we were there, to confer with or laugh with or just check if something was right. I was the keeper of all our memories now. I stood on the same stone floor that I had stood on when I was two, and I touched a wall on the veranda. The Indian air felt familiar on my skin. I was clutching my old photos and I showed some to the owner. "Your family?" he asked. "Deceased?" We were both in tears by then.

That house, where we went when I was two, was provided by the company, Tube Investments. It was spacious and comfortable, as were the other distanced houses on the road. Next to us was an empty plot with patchy dried-up grass and pink earth. Grey water buffalo roamed around looking for something to eat. When it rained the earth became muddy and a dip in the middle filled with water where the buffalo loved to wallow. I watched them up to their necks in thick pink water, happily sitting still. And then they tried to get up, heavily swaying and heaving and pulling to rise and walk away. The pink water sloshed and the suction of mud held them down. The process seemed to take hours, and their struggle went on and on. I thought I could see the beginnings of panic in their flat grey faces and wide-spaced staring eyes and that hint of panic began to become my own. Eventually they succeeded and I watched them walk away. Sometimes they wandered into our garden and ate Mum's precious cannas. "Quick quick. Shut the gate shut the gate." Our mali[7] had left it open.

Khader Nawaz Khan Road was a quiet road. There wasn't much traffic, but in those days there weren't many cars. There were bullock carts pulled by buffalo or cows, and long-handled carts with large, thin wheels which were pulled from the front and pushed from the back by men. On the slightest downward slope the man at the front had to steady and restrain the cart, holding its whole weight with his body. I worried it might suddenly pick up speed, start hurtling forward out of control, and crush him. On the upward incline the man at the back would bend double, his head and his hands pressed hard against the load, and with long strides and all the strength in his thin legs he would push upwards. The loads were massive and always very precarious – straw

---
7 *mali*: a gardener.

or cane or sacks of grain and things I didn't know the name of. The men wore loin-cloths and cloths wound around their heads. They covered their feet in sacking to protect them from the melting streets. Their dark brown skin was shiny and wet with the sweat of enormous effort.

There were hand-pulled rickshaws with whole families aboard and a few ambassador cars. Cows and people could safely stroll at leisure. Cowpats lay splattered on the ground and Ayah and I had to pick our way around them when we walked. When they dried they formed a crust which made them look quite solid. I jumped on one to test this out and a runny yellow mess, stinking and warm, shot up and coated my legs. I was utterly astonished, and Ayah was not amused. I remember the shock to this day and I am still respectful of cowpats. I also learnt that outer layers are often quite deceptive, not as safe or strong or solid as they may first appear. Who knows what softness lies beneath? We have to prod with care.

Nearly everyone chewed betel nut and paan leaves in those days. It seemed an incessant habit and now I know it was, for some, a harmful narcotic dependence. It appears to be less prevalent today. I walked with Ayah, and men and women chewed and smiled at me. I saw inside their mouths. I saw their blood-red teeth and juicy tongues with saliva overflowing. The betel nut bled its colour. People were good at spitting and projectile splashes were strewn on roads and stained the base of walls, in and outside buildings. The wet red turned pink as it dried in the sun and became OK to walk on. There are different paan concoctions, and paan-maker stalls are an artwork of ingredients. Heart-shaped leaves are stacked in kaleidoscope patterns and small metal pots contain intriguing pastes and slivers of surprises like lime or coconut or cloves. You can smell the cardamom and mint. You can watch the vendor's precision as he quickly creates these small and fresh green bundles with their peculiarly intricate taste.

Barrow sellers each had their regular pitch. They sold warm roasted peanuts in paper cones, crispy, spicy morsels and bright orange jelabis[8] which glistened with syrupy ghee. These sweetest of sweets were my favourites. The sugary juice oozed out when I bit through the outer edge. It covered my face and ran through my hands, and Ayah was thorough as she cleaned me up and tried to remove all trace. Food from the street could be risky and was strictly not allowed, but Ayah was always careful. She knew which sellers to choose.

8 *jelabi*: a fried coil of batter, steeped in syrup.

The house was only slightly set back from the road. It had a small front lawn with unpromising, usually half-eaten red cannas planted in a curve around it. There were two gates so you could drive in one and out the other, and a portico in the middle with the upstairs veranda on top. The kitchen area was three rooms – the first, nearest the dining room, for the fridge and storage, the next for cooking and then an area for washing up. They were warm and humid and had a distinctive odour, different from the rest of the house, of lingering food and drains. All drains had a strong, metallic rust smell. Sometimes I recognise it in the bathrooms of other hot countries and although not at all pleasant, its familiarity makes me smile. In the mornings my mum would stand by the fridge to discuss food and stocks with the cook and the bearer. Sometimes she did abracadabra and produced some sweets for me. Everything was screwed down tight and put away so that ants and other creatures couldn't eat it.

A small outside staircase led up to the flat kitchen roof, and then a few steps more led up to the bathroom attached to where I slept. Ayah had her own room downstairs at the back of the house. She kept her possessions there, her neatly folded clothes and her holy pictures and garlands with silver strands and bright coloured plastic flowers, shocking pink and green. She liked to have candles burning in small red glasses on a shelf. Ayah usually slept on the floor between my bedroom and bathroom. In the evenings she would sit on the back steps and chat with other ayahs, her friends. She was very clever. She could read and write in Tamil and in English and women would come to our house with words in their head for her to write into letters or letters in their hands for her to read. I lay in bed and heard their soft talking and laughing in the dark outside. Sometimes I was still awake when Ayah unrolled her bedding and lay down for the night.

We had a Gurkha nightwatchman. He arrived in the evening in his khaki shorts, thick socks and Gurkha hat. He brought with him his pole. Through the night you could hear him doing rounds of the house, thumping the pole as he walked. I think the thump was a warning to would-be burglars but also to scare away snakes. The rounds were intermittent, and sometimes I'd stay awake waiting for the regular, hollow, slowed-down heartbeat sound. I could picture him outside in the dark of our garden and walking behind our house, alone in the quiet night while I lay in bed and listened. I found it comforting and reassuring, not because of any security that he was supposed to supply but because of the repetition, the warm reliability of the sound. The Gurkha would be gone in the morning. I sometimes waved but I never spoke to him and I didn't know his name.

Travelling magicians sometimes stopped at our house and asked if they could perform their magic in our garden. Usually it was one man and his female assistant. There was no glitter or panache about the women; they dressed in an ordinary way and seemed to me to be rather old and tired. The man crouched on the grass, covered a pile of earth with a cloth and played his pungi horn to make a mango grow. Or he charmed a cobra out of a flat round basket and set it to fight a mongoose. I watched their bodies battle, horribly jerky and fast, until the mongoose won and the cobra lay still on the ground. The speed of the movement and the contrasting textures of their bodies, so furiously entwined, remain very clear in my mind. I don't think the death upset me.

My favourite trick was the woman in the basket. She was bound and tied in rope sacking and then lifted into a wicker basket, and she had to wiggle and squeeze and be pushed to fit in. The man put a sheet over the top, then the lid, and played his pungi horn. "Where is gone? To Calcutta? Where is gone? To Delhi?" Then he removed the sheet, keeping the lid firmly on. With great aplomb he then stuck a lengthy sword through the basket, several times in several directions. So where could the woman be?

Even the best contortionist couldn't have avoided that knife. The man played the pungi again – "Come back from Calcutta. Come back from Delhi" – and as he played, the lid began to rise. The woman's back became visible as, fully tied, she started to emerge from the basket into which she could hardly fit. The man lifted her out and untied her and both stood and took a bow. There were no trap doors in our garden, and I still don't know how it's done.

Opposite us was Doctor Somesekar. His wife had diabetes and had been through several amputations on her legs. I always hoped to see her, but rarely did, when we visited the surgery at his house. I pictured her decreasing legs and wondered how and where exactly all this chopping would end. I remember his voice as steady and reassuring and I remember high fevers and dysentery and enemas and freshly made coconut ice cream when I had my tonsils out.

Suzie Watkins lived a few houses away and was probably my best friend. She had blonde hair which people touched as we walked along roads with our ayahs. I had round cheeks which women would squeeze very hard and roughly twist with their fingers. I dreaded it because it hurt – but Ayah said it was a sign of affection, so I made myself let it happen. To this day I think my cheeks are bigger than they otherwise would be. The Watkinses had a white bull terrier called Tess. We loved her and we played with her in the garden, and I cuddled and kissed her and let her lick my face. I had been playing at their house one afternoon, and there was terrified panic when Tess died of rabies that night. Mrs Watkins said she had been "foaming at the mouth and snarling" before she died. They had shut poor Tess in the bathroom and I pictured her there turning in terrified circles, shredding herself and the walls. We had all been warned about rabies and the torturous death it caused. They didn't open the bathroom door until the next morning, when Tess had gone silent and they knew she was definitely dead. Poor darling Tess. I had many opportunities to see Mrs Somesekar after that, as I had fourteen injections in my stomach over the following weeks.

The Club

The library Mum went to was at the Adyar Club. We went there at least once a week – sometimes as a family, with Ayah, and sometimes just Mum and me. When we first went to Madras there was another club, more prestigious, called the Madras Club. Its members were mainly higher echelons of the British Raj or Army and it was very formal and starchy. No women or non-British men were allowed. Numbers dwindled through the fifties, and in 1963 it closed as a separate institution but blended itself into the Adyar Club, which was financially helpful to both. The Adyar Club had opened in the late 1800s specifically as a less formal option. It admitted women as guests, although not as members until many decades later. So the club I knew as the Adyar Club became the Madras Club, as it is now, and its address, rather oddly, is the Madras Club, Adyar

Club Gate Road. It was built by George Moubray, a wealthy employee of the East India Company, in the late 1700s. It was a garden house with enormous rooms and a great white cupola and acres of land and lawns sweeping down to the Adyar River.

In the fifties it was mainly a club for the British working in major companies in Madras – boxwallahs, as people in commerce were called. Many Indian writers, including VS Naipaul, mention boxwallahs; it is an interesting word with different meanings and connotations, but it was a slightly derogatory term, as being connected with commerce was less prestigious than being part of the elite of the Raj. The names of those companies still ring bells for me. I knew nothing about them, and still don't, but the words themselves feel familiar and pleasing to say: Binnies, Metal Box, Grindlays Bank, Avery's, Parry's, Ashok Leyland. My favourite was Metal Box. Such a simple and perfect name.

There were no or very few non-British members of the Club until the mid-fifties when other Europeans, such as diplomats and consultants, and Americans began to join. Indians were 'invited to join' during the time of transition when the British were leaving and all companies and institutions were being handed on. Now membership is almost exclusively Indian. Out of about one thousand members, only around forty are foreign – maybe American, Japanese or British. The foreign faces you occasionally see are usually in Chennai for work. They live in the city and visit the club to use the pool, which wasn't there when I was a child, or the walking track, or just to socialise and enjoy the oasis of green and birds and beauty.

There are twelve guest rooms at the Club and to be able to stay, or indeed even enter the grounds, you have to be 'recommended' by a member. We are lucky, and grateful, that our friend Ramesh makes it possible for us to stay. He became a member in the late 1960s and has been deeply involved ever since, including being club president in the 1990s. I struggle with complicated guilt about past and sometimes present British behaviour, but Ramesh and I think many of the current members seem very matter-of-fact and forgiving. Acknowledgement of wrong does help, I think, but theirs is still a very generous perspective. Ramesh Lulla, like MS Mutiah in his day, has boundless curiosity and love for the Club and enormous knowledge of its history. They have both written books about it, and I am honoured to have contributed in a small way with old photos and some of my recollections. The Club is immaculate today; the buildings, the grounds, and much of the early ethos are all cherished and meticulously maintained.

The sight of the club buildings has an extraordinary impact on me. The whiteness, the pillars, the cupola and the sweeping steps to the long veranda at the front, and the black and white marble flooring on the portico side, are all so beautiful to behold. But even more breathtaking than the sight are the feelings. A surreal familiarity. A time-travel experience. The strongest sense of myself at that early age, in that place, among the people who were in my world at that time.

I went with my mum in the afternoons. We drove past the portico to a small building where the office and the library still are today. Mum stocked up on books and I meandered between the shelves, enjoying the smell and the extraordinary neatness of all the lined-up spines. When I returned to that library in 2002 I found two books which my mum had signed for – William Hickey's *Memoirs* and John Masters's *Bugles and a Tiger*. Perhaps I had been there when she had chosen them and carried them back to the car. I looked at her familiar writing on the sign-out card and ran my finger along the 'M V Forsyth' written by her hand.

After the library, we had tea on the veranda, or bearers arranged cane chairs and tables on the lawn. I had a tall glass of juice which they called an orange cobla. I liked to drink it noisily through a straw. Sometimes we walked near the edge of the river. An occasional rowing boat would glide by from the Boat Club further along, and small groups of buffalo swam or just wallowed on the opposite bank. I wore a hat and I felt the sun on my skin.

The back of the Club, the portico side, felt different. Pots of plants formed walkways into dense shade. It felt secluded and secret with jungly trees and leafy shrubs which smelt of hot earth and freshly watered warm plants. There was an aviary with whole trees in it and a myna bird that could speak in English, Tamil and Hindi. I loved that part of the Club. Sometimes I went there with Ayah and we sat on a bench near the aviary. We sat in the damp heat without talking. The birds were quiet at that time of day, just sitting it out in the trees, and the air was still, too hot to stir, and if anything moved it was slowly.

There were children's parties and parties I didn't go to when my parents dressed up and I stayed at home with Ayah. There were lunch get-togethers when families met, and there were decorations at Christmas. My dad was Father Christmas one year and ho-ho-hoed from a cart pulled by bullocks through the grounds.

In 1961 the Queen and the Duke of Edinburgh visited Madras, and Mum and Dad were two of a dozen people presented at a big reception at the Club; Jan was among the other guests. The Club was carefully, very elegantly lit and adorned for that evening. My mum wore a Dior dress in dusky-pink Chantilly lace. It became known as 'The Dior' and was probably the most expensive dress she ever owned – but then, it was for a very special occasion. I'm wondering now how she purchased that dress. No online shopping then. Maybe she had it sent from England and altered if necessary in Madras. It is one of the things I can't remember asking her, so now I'll never know. Mum practised her curtsey a hundred times and was incredibly nervous. Photography was not allowed except by one official photographer but as enormous luck would have it, one of the photos he took of the line-up was of Dad being presented, holding the Queen's hand as he bowed, and Mum beside him looking gorgeous, her head turned slightly towards them, readying herself for her turn. I choose who I show that photo to. It is, at best, irrelevant to many people, and at worst, negatively 'royal' to some. It's the same with the MBE.

I am proud of my dad. He was not from a privileged background. He started as an engineering apprentice, and during the apprenticeship he met my mum, who was typing in the 'Goods In / Goods Out' department. But through sheer hard work and enthusiasm and by being prepared to take a few risks, he worked his way to being a director of a major company. In 1965 he was awarded an MBE for his work in industry in India and for humanitarian and charitable activities. He was the first chairman of the Association for the Blind of South India and the first person to employ blind people in the factories. Everything he did was what he wanted to do, and he was lucky that he had my mum to support his efforts and enable him to do it. They had several moves because of his work, and there were lengthy separations while she was in England for Jan and me or, in later years, because she chose not to accompany him on his two-month stints after he officially retired. I may not have known all the nuances or ramifications of these arrangements, but they seem to me to have worked well for them both. My mum used her time without him – she followed her many interests, in art and music and ballet, and did several 'appreciation' courses, lapping up all the information and going off to galleries and museums and concerts as part of them. She had many friends with whom I hope she could share her enthusiasm as well as sharing it with me. Years later, in Suffolk, she had a garden to develop and would be up in the early morning, digging and planting and totally loving her task. I still visit that village, almost frozen in time, and can still see the rockery she built and made so beautiful.

School and Mrs de Silva

I went to school every morning with Ayah by car or by rickshaw. The rickshaws were mainly hand-pulled, as the bicycle ones were new and still few and far between. The plastic seat of the rickshaw was always scorching hot. It could take the skin off your legs. Ayah would lay down a thick cotton cloth for us to sit on but the heat would still burn through. The rickshaws would be parked at a very steep angle until the handles were lifted, so it was almost impossible not to slide off your seat. The trying not to always made us giggle. The seats of the car had sturdy cotton covers so you wouldn't stick to the leather. They were pristine white and I had to be careful when clambering in not to mark them with my shoes.

My school was a long one-storey building, open-plan before its time. Each morning we lined up outside the building according to our classes, and marched to the brass-band music which Mrs de Silva had put on the record player. We had the same music every day. Class by class we marched up the stairs and across the veranda and into the space, empty of desks, called the hall. Towards one edge of this space was an enormous piano at which Mrs de Silva sat waiting for us to form a thick semicircle around her. Every day I maintained my march as we entered the building and turned on the lethally shiny red floors. Every day I feared I might fall. It was the humiliation rather than the risk of pain that worried me.

Mrs de Silva played a tune and we sang. I don't know what tunes she played, but they wouldn't have been religious; we were Hindus, Sikhs, Catholics, Muslims, Protestants, Jains, and probably others too. Discovery of religion was experience rather than learning. Special days or customs were incorporated into our normal lives. A girl in my class arrived one day with a completely shaven head. I sat behind her and studied her sore and extraordinary baldness. Just the day before she had had thick, shiny black hair. She was embarrassed and brave. I asked my mum about it when I got home, and she said it was to do with her religion. I'm not sure which religion that might have been. Maybe it was something less interesting.

My best friend at school was a Czechoslovakian boy

called Firko. I'm not sure if that's how his name was spelt, but that was how it was said. He was taller than me, bony, with tawny smooth skin and spiky light-brown hair. We huddled together talking instead of playing with the other children at breaks. I felt happy when I was with him, and I invented stories about us. In one of them we did a trapeze act at school with everyone watching and thinking how clever we were. I swung towards him in my silver outfit and he caught me and carried me up to his ceiling-high perch. The perch became a tree-house where we lived together, away from people and houses, me in my silver costume and him in his blue and green trunks. Happily ever after.

Mrs de Silva was even more special than Firko. She had very long nails which changed colour every day in shocking shades of pink and orange and red. Her glossy lips matched her nails. Her hair hung loose, shoulder-length and flipped up at the ends, which was interesting and unusual at that time. She wore earrings and necklaces and lots of bangles which clinked together when she wrote on the board. Mrs de Silva smelt of a perfect combination of heavy sweet flowers and cigarettes, so when I stood by her at her desk to read, I could feel her grownupness beside me. She wore saris in gentle, wispy colours and embroidered cholis to match. She had an attractive wedge of dark-cream fat between the bottom of her choli and the waist of her sari. It divided into two soft ridges when she sat.

My mum used to give me her empty perfume bottles, which I treasured and sniffed until there was no smell left. Perfume was not constantly being finished, so a fresh bottle was a rare and exquisite treat. Finally a bottle arrived, and I was sitting alone on my bed devouring its smell and dreaming my dreams when I suddenly had the most brilliant idea. Mrs de Silva! What better, more precious gift could I give her to show her how I felt? Ayah helped me with my careful, painstaking wrapping. I placed the package on the table beside my bed so I could watch it through the night while I tried to wait for tomorrow.

The next morning, I made it safe in my bag so my books and orange juice wouldn't damage the bow, and then I sat through lessons and waited and waited for break. And then I presented my gift.

Mrs de Silva received it with great dignity, just as I knew she would. She was smiling as she unwrapped it with her long and perfect nails. The bottle was in its original black and white cardboard container, with the name of the perfume written near the top and then the number 5. My stomach was squeezing with excitement as I watched her face light up. I could hardly bear the waiting for her to lift the small glass stopper out of the bottle and sniff the beautiful smell. She had begun to thank me as she removed the bottle from the box, stared at it and then removed its top.

"You are a very very silly little girl," she told me as she slowly placed the bottle on her desk. "That is a very stupid trick. Giving a person an empty perfume bottle. Never do such a stupid thing again." She spoke quietly as though trying not to scream or even cry. Mrs de Silva was very, very unhappy. "Now go away," she said.

As soon as she told me, I could easily see how very disappointing my present must have been. I felt so stupid not to have thought of it before. Looking back, her response was harsh, but Chanel No. 5 would have been a very special extravagance, much as it is today. The rise of her heart and then the fall would have been hard to manage. Mrs de Silva and I never fully recovered from that day, and even now I try to be careful with presents.

The Afternoon at Mette's House

Mette was much older than us and wasn't a friend, so I don't know why Suzie and I would have been at her house that day. Perhaps our parents had gone out together and left us in the care of her ayah? Mette was Danish and prettily blonde, with pale skin and blue eyes. She was twelve years old and seemed to us to be very grown-up in her teenage clothes and her make-up. She talked to us about sex and told us things that I could hardly believe. Why would anyone do that? Why would boys want you to? Mette explained that it was because they liked it – so if you did it, it made them like you. Suzie seemed to think all this made sense, but I was none the wiser.

That day, Mette took us up to the flat white roof of her house and made Swami, the bearer, take his trousers down.

We'd been talking in her room. It was blissfully

cool from the air conditioning and smelt of perfume and make-up. It was the most feminine room I had ever been in — nothing like my parents' room or Jan's or Suzie's or mine. The bedding and rugs were matching and silky and the colours were gentle and soft. She had a proper dressing table, kidney-shaped, with three mirrors. It had a glass top over dusky-pink satin fabric which was gathered at the edges and hung like a curtain to the floor. There was a gap in the middle where Mette could put her knees when she sat to apply her make-up. White china jars with pink tops and a pretty round box of powder were carefully arranged on one side. Beside the powder was a feathery white face puff. It was the lightest, softest and fluffiest thing I had ever seen. So soft, I thought, that you may not even feel it on your skin. I desperately wanted to touch it.

"Have you ever seen a penis?" Mette asked us. She was sitting on the edge of her bed, filing her nails. I concentrated on the leather manicure set which was open on the bed beside her. It had little compartments and loops where the different instruments could fit snugly and securely. I liked the way it was made. Useful and nice to look at.

I hadn't seen a penis, in the flesh. I knew Suzie had, because she had a brother and a dad who didn't mind walking around with nothing on. All I had to go on were Suzie's descriptions and drawings.

Mette told us to follow her upstairs, and once we were there she called Swami.

It was Suzie who tried to stop it. "He doesn't want to do it, Mette."

"He'll do it," said Mette.

It was afternoon, and the sun was so vicious that even the crows had stopped crowing. Swami stood some distance away, in bare feet on the scorching floor, wearing his loose white bearer's uniform. He was older than our parents, and I knew he had worked for the family since they had arrived, when Mette was five years old.

"No, missy. No. Please, missy."

"Come on, Swami. Just quickly. Quickly up and down to show us."

Swami stood in front of us with his arms hanging, helpless hands by his side. He stared back at Mette with panicky, muddled eyes.

"Come on, Swami, or I'll tell Mummy I saw you take the sugar and then you'll get the sack."

"Please, missy. No."

"Do it or I'll tell Mummy."

Swami pleaded and then surrendered. He undid his white trousers and let them drop to the ground. He wasn't wearing underpants and his jacket wasn't long enough to cover him, so the revelation was sudden, and he stood for whole seconds in front of us while we quietly stared.

I have never forgotten the enlightenment of that moment or the absolute misery it caused. I have felt too ashamed to have ever told anyone about it. Looking back now, I wonder how Mette knew so much and where she had learnt to exert such frightening power.

I should have walked away or spoken up instead of standing still and staying silent. The shame of not doing so stays with me to this day. At that time I didn't know the words 'humiliation' or 'power', but I still knew that something very bad was taking place on that roof. The disparity of power frightens me. Sometimes, on a whim, it can trickle down into ordinary life, such as bullying at work or from a group to a lone individual. The self-righteousness of the bully and the bravado of a gang. The cruelty of making someone feel weak. I know it's said that people only have the power you give them. I would like to believe that, but sometimes I feel really it just isn't true.

A Picnic at Sadras

My parents had very social lives, with parties and dinners in the evenings and sometimes during the day. They would come into my room to say goodbye, dressed up and smelling of perfume. I didn't worry about them leaving. I was happy to stay with Ayah.

At weekends, during the day, we went to the beach or to favourite places for picnics. We mainly went with the Newns family, whom we had met on the ship sailing out. Dorrie and George Newns were my parents' closest friends. They had two sons at school in England and a daughter, Fran – she was FN when we were together, and I was FF or Forcy. FN was a remarkable person. Fearless and physically brave, she was the absolute opposite of me. She loved sports, could whack the ball hard in cricket, could swim under crashing waves to far-out sandbars, run like the wind or get stuck into a tackle. I loved all her daring achievements. She was a few years older than me and for a while she was like a second big sister. With all her sport, she also had injuries, and she broke one leg several times. I'm not sure if it was related, but she developed cancer in that leg and at seventeen she had an amputation. We were all back in England by then, and she and her mum stayed with us the weekend before her operation. We rode the horse which was kept in a field nearby. I was scared and fell off but I was happy to watch FN jump on and gallop fast and free. After they left, my mum told me what they would be facing that week.

Fran became an inspirational role model for Roehampton Hospital, for other young people facing the trauma of losing a limb. As soon as she was used to her prosthetic leg, she wanted to be active again. They filmed her ice-skating and horse-riding and she even crossed a desert on a camel, in Morocco I think. Mum explained how Fran had had to take changes of leg and special padding to protect the stump; she said in that heat the prosthetic could have rubbed her flesh raw. Those details conjured strong images for me, and still do. When she was older, Fran — by then known as Frances Hay — started the charity Dogs for the Disabled, which was registered in 1988 and is still thriving today as Dogs for Good. I picture her clear face and strong blue eyes as a child, and I see her when she was unwell when we were all at her mum's funeral. Fran died when she was forty years old.

The best place for picnics was an old Dutch fort at Sadras. It was about an hour's drive away, now more than two because of the terrible traffic. Sometimes the Turners came with us and we each drove in separate cars. George Turner was a friend of Dad's from work. I always opted to go with the Newnses so I could be near Fran and their dog, Nicky. Nicky was sometimes sick in the car, which wasn't so good, especially in the heat, but the risk was worth it for the other big lure of travelling with the Newnses. Fran's dad, George, was a British Trade Commissioner, which meant he had access to Spangles and other rare English sweets, and Fran's mum would hand these out on the journey. Such a treat to unwrap the coloured paper from each individual small square. I never minded which colour I had, although I particularly liked the green ones. They were literally mouth-wateringly fruity and deliciously sharp and sweet. I liked the thin bit in the middle which disappeared first so you could poke your tongue right through.

The cars were loaded with rugs and cushions and makeshift barbecue gear. There were ice boxes full of drinks and food, and the paraphernalia for cooking.

Cutlery and glasses were wrapped in cloths, and there were metal plates with segments for different food which Dad borrowed from the factory canteen.

In the 1600s, that Coromandel Coast was fraught with foreign powers. They built forts, set up trading posts and fought battles to gain control. The British East India Company was in Madras, based at Fort St George; the Dutch were at Sadras; the French at Pondicherry;[9] and the Danish in Tranquabar.[10] The ruins of the forts are all still there, except in Pondicherry, as the British destroyed it in 1761. But the French legacy remains strong there. It is an extraordinary enclave in Tamil Nadu where almost everyone speaks French. They have gendarmes, not police, and you can eat perfect croissants for breakfast.

At Sadras we parked outside what remained of the entrance, and with the help of people from the local village we each carried something to where we would set up our camp. Usually we aimed for the elephant stand with the shade of some trees and ruined walls which were good for resting plates on. There was a quiet, ghostly feel in the fort – a vast abandoned area of broken buildings, dark dungeons and small red bricks scattered on the dusty, pale

---
9   now Puducherry.

10   now Tharangambadi.

earth. Our voices and presence seemed to make little impact; they were superimposed, as we were, on that strange, ear-pulsing silence which heat and emptiness give off. It seemed a place that had been completely forgotten. I walked with my mum around the small Dutch cemetery – she felt it important to acknowledge the people there – and we tried to decipher the writing on the beautifully engraved flat stones. Sadras is now a heritage site, maintained by the Archaeological Survey of India, but in all the times I have been there over the last nearly twenty-five years I have never seen another visitor. It remains a deserted, abandoned Dutch fort, full of its own history and a vivid part of mine.

The men did the cooking, with numerous G&Ts and beers, while we lounged on rugs, chatting, eating freshly cooked, salted cashews and drinking tea or ice-cold sweet limes. I have a black-and-white photo of us in hot sunlight and patchy shade. Jan is lying on cushions and I'm sitting beside her with a hat skew-whiff on my head. I think it belonged to FN. Mum, sitting behind me and wearing dark glasses, is looking away at something outside our group. Flo Turner is probably talking, the sun on her arms, and I am smiling at her. I remember a blouse she often wore. It had short cap sleeves with patterns cut out in the shape of tiny flowers. When the sun shone through, it left petal-shaped shadows on her arms. I think of Flo Turner whenever I see broderie anglaise.

The men produced an enormous lunch with hundreds of different components – it was really a supersized English breakfast. They would be hot and laughing and noisy from all the drinks mixed in with the sun and the heat of cooking. We ate our lunch and then maybe the adults dozed for a while before a game of cricket. I never joined in but happily watched as FN outran them all.

My favourite bit was the sea. We girls wandered off to one of the large and only slightly collapsed constructions which we used as a changing room. There were several around the grounds, perhaps granaries or dining halls in their day. With swimming costumes in hand we would pick our way over the dry, stony ground and low remains of walls, through the piercing heat and bright sunlight. The ceiling of the building we chose was still intact, as were most of the walls, so it was deeply shady inside and it took a while for our eyes to adjust to the darkness. It felt cool but humid and the air had a strong musty tang. Looking up, we saw hundreds and hundreds of bats silently hanging from the ruined ceiling, their brown shapes tightly packed together, blending into the gloom. I didn't like the bats. I was afraid they would suddenly take flight and get tangled in my hair, because someone had told me that is what bats do. There were occasional twitches of movement but generally the mass of live bodies stayed still.

Further on from our changing room, across more dry earth and rubble, was the external wall of the sea side of the fort. Once we'd clambered over it, we were on the wide beach of pale sand next to the crashing Indian Ocean. We kept our shoes on right up to the water's edge as the sand was too scalding to walk on.

The waves of the Indian Ocean were not for the faint-hearted. They could suck you under or dislocate your shoulder if you didn't time things right. FN would be making her way to the sandbar we knew was there, while the rest of us held on to a hand or shrieked with joy as we jumped and fell in the shallows. Even at the edge, the waves were strong and could knock you flat and drag you along on your stomach, filling your costume with sand – a peculiar, heavy feeling, which I didn't like. Further out, you couldn't withstand the strength of a wave – all you could do was swim under. I learnt to do this at a very young age but still felt afraid sometimes that I would run out of breath before the thick mass of water had thundered over and passed me. Beneath its strength I would wait and wait for it to move forward so I could emerge and gasp for air in the space of flat sea behind. I would watch it head for the shore while I stocked up on breath for the next one. Getting back to the beach could be troublesome – riding the wave and then battling the undertow, that determined pull to drag you out to sea. Unlike FN, I didn't go too far, and I knew an adult would be there to grab me if I needed to be pulled back to safety. Jan stayed at the edge of the sea. Dad or George or one of the other adults usually held her hand. Too much of a wave could unsteady her and she would fall, and although she would laugh with genuine glee there was also an edge of worry. She wouldn't be able to right herself on her own.

My sister had cerebral palsy. I never ever thought of her as having something 'wrong' – rather, there was just something slightly different which I hardly ever thought of at all. It affected her right side. She walked with a limp and her right hand was clenched and her right arm wouldn't do what she wanted. Sometimes the right side of her mouth would rise as if smiling and she'd use her left hand to hold it straight. When she was upset or anxious, her speech was affected and her arm would flail, and she'd hold it still with her 'good' hand. At home, when she was relaxed and happy, her movements were calm and easier for her to manage. Jan was a natural giggler. She found things very funny and was interested and bright and vivacious. At that time, it would not have occurred to me that she ever struggled or grappled with the image others had of her, or had to work hard to fit in. In those days, the word was 'spastic'. As far as I know, it wasn't derogatory then – or perhaps I just couldn't imagine that anyone would use it that way.

After our swim we would all troop back over the wall and across the grounds to the ancient well, which still contained fresh water. One by one we stood while one of the men pulled at a rope to raise the holey bucket. The water felt clean and cold and made us scream as we washed the salt away. I'd copy Jan, pulling my costume away from my skin so the water would go down my front. My big sister was beautiful-looking. Something of Princess Margaret, when the princess was at her best – the dark hair and blue eyes and full mouth. But when Jan was having water poured over her at the well at Sadras, her laughter and expressions were more like Marilyn Monroe. Her gorgeous shape in her green swimming costume, her head back and face towards us, laughing and laughing with the shock of the drenching and the cold. We dried off in the sunshine, drank cups of tea and went home.

Lady Bountiful

At Christmas, driver would take me in the car to his home, just the two of us. It was a very special event. I sat on the cotton-covered front seat beside him, bathed and meticulously dressed. My lap was covered by a large open box containing ten bags of assorted sweets, each carefully wrapped by Mum in green cellophane paper and tied with wide red ribbon. The paper was stiff, shiny and transparent and it had a Christmassy feel. As we drove, we chatted easily. I liked our driver and felt comfortable being with him.

I know now this was very 'Lady Bountiful' of me, and even then I worried that this was how it would seem. But I didn't feel bountiful, and driver and his wife and children never gave me the impression that they thought I felt I was. I just wanted to deal with my shyness. I wanted to be friendly and polite.

I carried the big box into the small two-roomed house. The rooms were dark and there were a lot of children. The youngest was lying in a hammock suspended from the ceiling. I thought this was a fascinating idea – not only did it seem a comfortable bed, but it saved floor space and kept the child completely out of the way. The second youngest was in his mother's arms. She offered him to me to hold, and I knew I was supposed to be thrilled. I had to put my box of sweets on the floor and take the child. He felt heavy. He smelt of skin and I held him awkwardly, afraid I might drop him. Once I thought I had smiled enough and held him for a reasonable time, I handed him back to his mother, the other children watching me. Then I picked up my box and presented it to the mother. She smiled appreciatively and distributed the shiny green bags of sweets. All the children seemed excited.

I stayed at driver's house for about fifteen minutes. He was our interpreter from Tamil to English – although I did know some words in Tamil, especially terms of endearment used for children. I wasn't offered anything to eat or drink, but I knew this was intentional and a matter of courtesy, as anything I wasn't used to might put my young English stomach on the brink.

Afterwards driver took me back home and we

talked about his children. I felt very contented with the event and looked forward to telling Mum all about it. He would leave the car at our house and go all the way back to his by bus. The following day was Christmas Day and he had two days off.

These episodes with the sweets happened several Christmases running, and my memories of them are clear and good and strong. But now I feel awkward at the thought of myself as that small child bestowing bounty. I know my mum's intentions were good and am fairly certain the carefully wrapped sweets were received with a lot of pleasure. But it's hard to know where to place these events. It's hard to know what to think.

A Sailor is Just for Christmas

British Merchant Navy ships sometimes docked at Madras. Normally, I suppose, the sailors were left to their own devices, but at Christmas it was felt they should be welcomed by local British people and included in family life and festive goings-on. I don't know how many sailors make up a crew, but I would think it was a lot more than there would have been British families. Perhaps the lucky ones were chosen by rank and the others had to stay on their ship.

Our sailor that year was called David. I liked him very much. Jan was in love with him, just as she'd been in love with Ron the year before and with Simon the year before that. Sometimes I could see her practising faces in the bathroom mirror. She would smile and flick her hair and pretend to smoke, the way that actresses did. Her dress for the evening would be hanging on the outside of her cupboard and the layers and layers of frilly petticoat would be fluffed up white and ready on the end of her bed. They looked as light as the feathers of baby birds which she would not let me touch. She would carefully sit at the top of her bed listening to her records. Dreaming, I suppose, of David. Almost every evening for nearly two weeks, my parents took David to a party and Jan, who was nearly seventeen, would sometimes be allowed to go too. I don't think David and Jan were ever alone together, so as far as I know any romance was confined to the dreams in her head. He was young, probably only in his early twenties, and far from his home and his family. He did well to fit so comfortably into ours. In the day, we all did things together, and I think he liked that best. Perhaps he found it easier when I was there as well. "We'll practise your dives tomorrow," he said, while I stood with Ayah and waved as they drove away for their evening. I think it was a thought to hang on to just as much for him as it was for me. I liked David, the way he spoke to me in a normal voice instead of the one that adults use with children. I liked the way he held my eyes when he spoke and listened properly when I answered.

Suzie's sailor was about the same age as David, but I thought he was far more handsome. His name was

Andrew, and he was very tall and had thick brown hair and brown eyes. Suzie hardly ever saw him as he spent his time with her parents in the evenings and mainly with her mum in the day. Sometimes he was there in the afternoons when I went to her house to play. We saw him and Suzie's mum talking in their downstairs room, their heads tilted towards each other as if struggling to catch the words; he was watching her mouth carefully, perhaps trying to see what she was saying. On a table near them, tall glasses of fresh lime seemed to have been forgotten. The ice had melted and the sugar had sunk to the bottom. Later, when they had gone to another part of the house, Suzie and I drank what was left in the glasses. It was horribly warm and bitter and made my teeth go on edge.

Having a sailor to look after made life extremely busy. We showed him all the important sights in the city and took him to beaches and clubs and for drives along the coast. We wandered around temples and markets. Usually my mum would be exhausted by going to parties night after night and moving around by day in the dreadful heat, which she said was utterly wilting. Mum hated the heat. She said she could hardly bear it. She talked about heat as if it were a place, waiting for her outside the windows of an air-conditioned room. But at this time of year it wasn't too bad, and she seemed happy to look after David.

The best place for me was the Gymkhana Club, where we used to go to swim and where David taught me to dive. When I was much older I had a dog called Sam. He was a springer spaniel, and as our car neared his favourite walk he would be almost ill with excitement. That's how I felt on the drive to the Gymkhana Club. We went along a big main road and turned right just after a statue. Just the sight of the statue made my happiness too big to fit. It made me feel quite sick. I would be let out by the entrance, before the car was parked, so I could run towards the pool, smell the water and see the blue as I ran up the spiral staircase, along the veranda to the ladies' changing room.

I could spend the whole day going in and out of the water. I had to be made to eat and drink and just sit still for a moment. We sat under cover at metal tables, and crows perched on the edges of chairs nearby; we had to flap them away. The Club did fat golden chips with tomato ketchup, and thick ice-creamy milkshakes. The hot and cold, the salt and sweet was delicious, and to have them by the pool with a whole afternoon still to go was absolute paradise to me.

When Jan had been about the age that I was then, they were living in Calcutta. They spent time at a pool, and that was where Jan learnt to swim. Mum and Dad and their friends and hers all cheered her on as she completed her first width. Afterwards they had a small party in celebration, and Mum arranged for a cake. She asked Jan what she would like written on it, and Jan said, "Congratulations to Janet for swimming a width of the outside pool." I think of those words as her epitaph. Luckily it was a big cake.

When the sailors were leaving, they held a lunchtime party on their ship as a thank you to all their hosts. We all dressed up and my dad said how lucky he was to have three such beautiful girls. We were quiet in the car as we drove to the harbour on the other side of the city. I felt sad that David was leaving. Jan kept moving her head and flicking her hair, which she did when she was nervous. She would have known that getting onto the ship would be a very tricky process.

When we arrived at the harbour, we had to stop as a long metal bar blocked our way, and a man came out of a box at the side of the road to see who we were before he would let us through. He was in a uniform with a hat and high woollen socks without feet, and his shorts were enormously wide and pointed and reached down to his knees. His legs jutting out made me laugh, which made Dad cross. I think he was worrying about parking.

We parked a long way from the ship and had to walk on uneven ground, past crates and cranes and other ships, to get to where our sailors were waiting. People were standing by the edge of the water. Some were guests like us, in daytime party clothes, and then there was David and Andrew and other sailors wearing white uniforms and hats. They looked as clean and perfect as their ship, which was moored a little way out. As it was our last day together my dad had brought his camera and he took a photo of David with Jan wearing his hat at an angle, then another one of the four of us together. The ship we were aiming for looked huge. We had to clamber into a small motor boat which took us out to the ship, then climb up ladder-type steps to the deck. I don't know how Jan managed it. Despite her laughter, she must have been anxious, but she would have made the most of the eager help of lots of handsome sailors.

The ship smelt of sea, burning dust and oily engines all mixed and vibrating together. The room where we ate was thick with smoke and perfume. Music was playing and voices were loud and it all made me feel a bit queasy – Suzie and I had eaten everything we could see. I went outside and looked across the water towards our part of the city. That was where Ayah would be, and I wished I was there with her in our ordinary house on a street instead of on a ship on the sea.

Everyone got noisy, and climbing down the ladder and into the small boat seemed a lot funnier to them all than it had done on the way out. At the front of the boat my dad and Mr Watkins and other men were laughing and shouting in a loud and brittle way. I was at the back on a low wooden bench, wedged between Mrs Watkins and the side of the boat, which was just low enough for me to rest my chin on. Mum and Jan were in front of me with Suzie by their side. I turned to speak to Mrs Watkins and saw that Andrew's hand was very lightly holding the top of her arm. They were not talking and were both looking towards the men at the front. They seemed tired, and I'd forgotten what I wanted to tell her, so I turned away to look at the sea instead.

We walked back to our car. David and Andrew and other sailors were standing beside the water. The Watkinses were driving away, and Mrs Watkins was looking back through the window. I turned to wave to them all and saw Andrew was watching their car. He wasn't smiling, but he was waving goodbye.

The next day, I imagined the empty space where the enormous ship and all those people had been. It was unsettling that something so substantial could be there one day and then quite simply be gone.

How We Got to Kodai

Jan's school holidays spanned Christmas, the visit of sailors and at least a month each side. A lot of children her age were at boarding schools in England but a separation of that distance would not have worked for Jan. So she went to Presentation Convent in Kodaikanal, otherwise known as PCK. It was an extraordinary school, tucked away 7000 feet above sea level in the Palani Hills. Its pupils came from families all over India — British, European and Indian. Mother St John was in charge throughout Jan's years at the school. She was open-hearted and open-minded and her energy and intelligence ensured the highest standards of care and education, not only academically but in social values and in the arts and music too. The school was a centre of excellence for music, and exams were held in association with Trinity College of Music. The order of nuns was the Presentation Sisters, and they are still present across the globe. The fees received from institutions like PCK pay for their work with the poor in countries all over the world, including areas in Britain. They consider themselves to be educationalists, not missionaries, and they respect other faiths and make provision for them.

When Jan first went to PCK, we all went up by car and we stayed for a week at the Carlton Hotel to see her settled in. I don't remember that first occasion or exactly which month it was, but I know from Mum how heart-rending it was to leave her there and drive back down to the plains. I think that first stint would have been for several weeks. She came back home for the Christmas break in October and her speech had deteriorated badly, and the distress of coping with that new situation was clear. I can understand my parents' dilemma; the school was right for Jan, it was caring, educationally good and could meet her needs, but the distance and separation were emotionally too much for her.

With the help of Mother St John, they arrived at a brilliant solution. Mum and I would live in Kodai for five months a year so that, together with the month's holiday at mid-term, when we'd all be together in Madras, Jan would never have more than a few weeks there without us. Lisieux Cottage was a typical, stone, Kodai house which the nuns would let us rent. It was just across a lane within a few minutes of the school. Jan was perfectly happy with that arrangement. So was Mum, as instead of enduring the unbearable heat in the plains, she was able to live in Kodai, her absolute paradise on earth. Dad drove up most weekends. He and our driver shared the driving, and if they left Madras early on Friday afternoon they would usually arrive by midnight. Theirs would be the only car on the ghat road[11] at that time of night, and Mum could see the lights across the dark valley when they were half an hour away. He'd stay until Sunday lunchtime. Only my parents used our driver's name, which I think was Vinoo. In a topsy-turvy way it was considered more respectful for me, as a young child, to call him 'driver' than it would have been for me to use the familiarity of his name.

I think Jan came and went with the other girls from the school, some of whom became her lifelong friends. They would have converged from their various places around India and even further afield, and then caught the train from Madras to Kodai Road Station. From there they would have been driven the fifty miles or so up the winding ghat road. Jan told us that on the way down they would all look out of the window and say, "The plains, the plains, the beloved

11 Ghat roads were constructed, mostly during the British Raj, to connect hill stations in mountainous regions of India. See https://en.wikipedia.org/wiki/Ghat_Roads.

plains," and on the way back they would look up at the range above them and say, "The hills, the hills, the beloved hills!" I say this out loud on our journeys up and down now, and I always think of Jan.

Mum, Ayah and I would get the sleeper which left Madras at around 9.00 p.m. and arrived at Kodai Road Station in the early hours of the morning. The train, which is still running and which I have used several times, is called the Pandian Express. Dad and driver would drive through the night and meet us at the station, and we'd pile in together with all the luggage for the rest of the drive up the ghats. We had a sleeper berth on the train with a small toilet attached. Mum and Ayah went round with Flit and Dettol before we set off, and then we settled in.

I loved those journeys. Everything so totally train-like with the metal beds and shelves above and the tiny basin and three-layered windows and the rushing around and noise of the crowd in the station. The carriage and surfaces all smelt of warm metal and there was a dusty smell, comfortable and creamy. We sat on our clean bedding with our luggage arranged and our picnics and lots of water and juice in a chill box ready beside us. Boiled eggs and curry puffs. The smell burst out when you took the wrapping off. The windows had horizontal bars on the outside, then a wire mesh blind to keep out insects and slatted shutters to close through the night. I can't remember if there was glass or air conditioning, but I don't think there was either. The train moved off, and once out of the city it would be pitch-black outside. I'd fall asleep tucked up in a bunk but would wake in the night when we stopped at stations, because the wheels made a loud screeching sound which lasted for several minutes. It seemed to take a very serious struggle for our train to come to a halt. I'd see the lights through the slats on the windows and the shadows of hands or the shapes of passers-by. It was eerie to hear the disembodied voices from outside. The yelling was distant, then loud, then faded away as the sellers made their way down the platform. They yelled the name of snacks I wasn't allowed and repeatedly shouted, "Chai chai. Chai chai."

We arrived in ghostly morning light, when the night still wasn't quite finished. Dad and driver were waiting, and we'd stretch our legs and then begin the drive. For the first half-hour the road was flat and quite straight with acres of coconut groves on both sides. The trees were planted in perfect rows with astonishing, pleasing symmetry. Even now I'm transfixed by the perfection of those lines. The villages we passed were half-asleep and the few people we saw seemed quiet and slow — lighting a fire, pouring water, walking towards a shrine. Then we arrived at the base of the ghats, the start of our upward journey. Nearly two hours of constant hairpin bends. You could not overtake. You could not see what was coming. There were wild forests and banana plantations and waterfalls with names. Occasionally we drove through small villages with wood-and-dung fires smoking. People were wrapped in coarse woollen shawls, still sleepy in these first chilly hours of their day. They laid out their vegetables and arranged their produce for sale. Dogs and cows, chickens and small ponies roamed around as our car drove slowly through, and families of small grey-brown monkeys sat on the low walls and watched us pass in the hope we would throw them some food. Invariably I would feel sick, and every half-hour we would have to find a safe stretch to stop so I could walk with Mum until I felt less green. At the beginning of this journey we could see the plains beneath us, but as we passed Snake Falls in the distance and continued our climb, there was just forest and sheer drops and white wild flowers and endless folding hills. The temperature changed as we climbed higher, and by the Jesuit shrine we'd need to put on our cardigans. The air felt cool here, and smelt different. It smelt of cows and woodsmoke and the tall and silvery eucalyptus, blue gum trees. At Silver Cascades we knew we were nearly there. We stopped and got out of the car. We watched and heard the thundering water crash over the rocks high above us and under the road where we stood, and we watched it emerge on the other side and rush down deep into the valley, eventually out of our sight.

We left the car by Lisieux Cottage and walked across the lane, through the chocolate gate – a wooden gate painted brown – and up the steps to get Jan. She was excited and happy to see us and to start her life as a 'day girl'. It would be the perfect, manageable mix of living with her family but being close enough to the school to stay involved in everything her friends and her classmates were doing. The school was unique in all its activities, and it was a social life for us all.

There was no expectation that Ayah would want to stay in Kodai. She could have stayed with the household in Madras; she had family there, a married daughter, and the climate in Kodai was very different from the plains. But Ayah always chose to be with us, and over the months we were there, over several years, she established her Kodai way of life, her friendships and routines, as we did. A local young woman called Rosie helped in the house, and she and Ayah became the best of friends.

So we had our very female household and settled into our lives in what I think was then one of the most beautiful places on the planet.

Kodai Life

Days were mainly sunny, like a hot English summer's day but clear and sharp and sparkling. There were bright red flowers against a bright blue sky. Evenings and early mornings could be cool. Sometimes it rained and rained and the whole of Kodai smelt green and damp and everywhere was heavily perfumed. There was jasmine and honeysuckle and roses. There was mist which descended and hid the view. It hid Perumal.

The Kodai mist has descended and people are lost in forests where there used to be bears and tigers and are perched on the edge of rocks, afraid to move, unsure of where they are. Monkeys scrabble on tin roofs, rain hammers down, and waterfalls and streams become noisy. Streets are alive with frogs. Be careful where you tread.

Perumal is Kodai's own mountain, flat-topped

and always visible in the distance if not shrouded in mist. In the early mornings you stood above the cloud – thick and white and solid enough for me to think it would easily take my weight. Flat cloud in the mornings, with strong apricot edging and Perumal rising above. Wrapped up against the clean chill, looking out and hearing Kodai.

Hill ranges at such mountainous heights exude a noisy silence. Perhaps it's just pressure in the ears, light-headedness from the thin air. But soon the sounds became more grounded – dogs barking, bells on cattle, people talking, an occasional passing car. Sound travelled. Tinny Tamil music blared from a marriage hall and bounced across streets and valleys.

Kodai houses were strewn across the hillsides and along the edge of the lake. They all had names that everyone knew by heart – Orchard House, Fernleigh, Rock Cottage, Woodstock. They had sturdy, thick stone walls and corrugated, steep-slanting roofs and front porches the length of the house. The upper half of the porch was all windows so you could see the view and enjoy the light and the sunshine. A conservatory-type porch, a closed-in veranda. Some had open verandas with overhang roofs with decorative wooden edging. The paintwork was usually green. There are various paints that colour, which I now call Kodai Green; my stomach jolts with pleasure when I see it as my memory nerves are touched. The houses had gardens, carefully, lovingly tended. The flowers and plants were visibly happy in the Kodai sun and rain and they smelt as all plants should do, of exactly what they were. Roses smelt strongly of roses, even the most delicate ones. Today, when I smell the powerful, sweet fragrance of box shrubs I am transported entirely, in body and time, to a beautiful damp Kodai day.

The houses were mainly on one level. Ours had a small living room with an open wood fire and two simple bedrooms, one with the bathroom leading off. We had a metal bath, and water was heated in pans on a fire at the back. Ayah put scrunched-up eucalyptus leaves into the warm bath water which made the room smell like Vicks. She said it was good for our skin. It could be perishing cold in Kodai throughout the winter months, but those weren't the months we were there.

Kodai was a 'Jewel in the Crown' type of hill station, and when we were there it had been used as such for about a hundred years. There was another school, High Clere, originally started many decades earlier for the children of American missionaries. There was a church, a bank, a boathouse, a club. There was a shop called Spencer's, by the lake. A one-storey brick building under a corrugated roof, it sold everything from shampoo to shoes. It had a soapy smell with a base note of warm vanilla from the fresh cakes they made there daily. There was a bazaar and a busy market full of stalls and mysteriously well-stocked shops. Buildings were bumpy and uneven. They were made of mud and painted in bright colours – green and turquoise and orange. The post office had lumpy white walls and high-gloss green and red paintwork. It had a homely feel.

Most roads led to the lake. The edges were thick with lilies which we could touch when Dad rowed us out in a boat. I loved their pale buttery colour and the way they opened and closed. There were very few cars, and when Dad wasn't there with ours, our only option was walking. Some of the walks took hours. Some were just for the pleasure of walking, and some were to shop or to visit the people Mum knew. They all involved a steep climb up or down and usually crossed a stream, gushing or quiet. Sometimes we took off our shoes and tucked up our skirts and paddled across. The water was clear and icy and we had to be careful which rocks we picked to stand on. There were paths through lumpy grassland and through forests of pine and cedar and through the blue gum trees. The gum trees were toweringly tall.

Ayah and I went for walks or played in the garden. She would be my 'patient patient' and let me bandage her arm or nurse her through high fevers. We played houses with complicated floor plans made of stones, and hide and seek, and pupils and teachers when I had to tell her off. I sat at the back of the house while she and Rosie pottered. I saw Rosie kill chickens; she broke their necks and then she chopped off their heads. There was a special stone for her to lay their necks on. Ayah would go to the market and come back with lots of news, telling me and Mum what she'd seen and who she'd spoken to. She often grumbled and she had a low opinion of most men. "He's just a good for nothing," she would say.

When I was old enough, perhaps at five, I went to PCK during the months we were there. Jan and I would come and go together through the chocolate gate and up and down the steps. We both looked smart in our uniforms. I learnt my times tables there, which we had to recite like a poem. "Four times one is four. Four times two is eight." The teacher went round the class, and I became more and more anxious about the sound of my voice and that I'd forget the table I had learnt the previous evening and practised so hard to say. The girl before me was nearly halfway through. My dread started building. I was next in line, waiting, and suddenly I just couldn't do it. I ran from the room and through the school and across the ground at the front, past all the plants, down the steps, through the chocolate gate and over the road to our house. To this day I hate the closing-in of the circle, waiting your turn to have to speak when the choice is out of your hands. I want to run away.

Jan's best friend was Flis Gibson, who lived with her parents in Shamrock, just a few minutes' walk from us. Flis's mum, Mrs Gibson, taught music at PCK. She had grey hair which she wore in plaits, pulled up and over her head. Flis was skinny and naughty; she and Jan were full of giggles and laughter and secret talks which I think were to do with boys. The Gibsons' cat had kittens, which I loved to cuddle and stroke. One day, Jan came home aghast. She had just watched a python eating one of the kittens. It had stayed complete, she said – just one big lump as it moved down the python's body.

Jan sang in the school choir – not very well, but they put her next to strong singers so she wouldn't put others off. She said she was a 'messy soprano'. She used to sing in the back of the car, emotional, made-up operatic arias which really amounted to a scream. She did it louder and louder, which made me laugh, until Dad said that was enough. Sometimes friends from her class came to our house for picnic lunches. I have photos of them with me, nine years younger, sitting on someone's knee. The girls are mid-sentence and mid-smile, in summer dresses, with a sandwich or a glass of juice in their hands. Our garden is drenched in sunlight and looks like a meadow, with an orchard and the shapely green Kodai landscape behind.

I did ballet. Miss Dupont, who had a strong French accent, was our teacher. She wore flesh-coloured, French teaching ballet shoes with a heel. I'd wanted to be a ballerina from the age of three and my heroine was Clare Black, one of the senior girls. Clare was a true ballet dancer and went on to dance professionally in her adult life. She may have been fifteen when she did the Dying Swan. The music and her movements were unbearably beautiful, and at my young age they took my breath away. I imitated her dance on a large mat in front of our house; Mum must have had the music and she put the record on. There is a rather lengthy cine film of me going back and forth on the mat. I am wearing a dress my mum will have made, with a net skirt that I stop every so often to puff up and arrange. I raise my arms and point my toes and look down sadly when injured. I hop back and forth on one leg. I want to replicate the beauty that Clare bestowed on this dance. I kneel on one leg with the other outstretched, I bend, I arrange my skirt just one more time for the grand finale. I die.

Every year each school house produced a ballet. I was in St Xavier's and was always chosen to be in ours, even if only in the background. I practised hard and loved being part of the show. As long as I didn't have to speak, I was happy to be on stage.

A lot of our life centred around the school. There was a pool in the woods which we could use for swimming, but it was far too icy to enjoy. There were music recitals, ballets, plays, sports days and regular film shows. People from outside could go to see the films. At one time Sheikh Abdullah of Kashmir, known as the Lion of Kashmir, was under house arrest at a house called Kohinoor just up the hill from our cottage. Nehru had had him imprisoned. There were security men and armed guards and a sentry at his gate. He and his wife and daughter sometimes went to film shows or special events at the school, accompanied by his guards, and he and Mum would wave to each other if she saw him when she walked past the house. She said he was very gracious.

The nuns weren't shut-away innocents; they had histories, interests and talents that they were happy to share. Some had travelled widely, and they had funny stories to tell. Mum enjoyed their company, as did Dad. Mum met Father Jim, a Jesuit priest who used to visit the convent. He'd come to our house and they sat for hours discussing the existence (or non-existence) of God and the meaning (or non-meaning) of our lives. They wrote to each other for many years and I still have some of his letters. Mum also studied French at the school to O-level standard and was as anxious, and then happy, as the rest of the class when the results came through.

Dad came at weekends, sharing the drive with our driver, and sometimes brought friends with him, like Mary MacGukin who worked as a secretary for him. I've known Mary since I was two. She is nearly ninety now. Her Indian mum and Scottish dad lived in Whitefields, near Bangalore[12], but she had grown up in the north. Mum and Dad were friends with her parents and her grandad, who died aged 103. Mary moved to England in her twenties and we have always been in touch, sharing various stages of our lives. She had the softest hands I've ever known, beautifully perfumed with Revlon Aquamarine hand lotion. I don't think it's made any more.

The Newnses quite often visited and we'd drive off to special spots for picnics — Dorrie's Dell, Basil's Boulders, George's Gorge, Fran's Folly (I think that was named for FN). I can't remember the ones for me or Jan or Molly. We went shopping. We visited friends and had tea on their verandas. I rode ponies

---
12 now Bengaluru.

round the lake – "Up down up down," the man would say over his shoulder as he led the pony round. And I spent time with Ayah.

At the end I had special lessons in pounds, shillings and pence. I sat with a nun in a music room which overlooked the large outside playground and tried to understand what she was attempting to explain. "You're going to need to know this," she kept saying. "Just some idea of the money they use over there." She must have had infinite patience, because I know I didn't grasp the idea. I barely had the hang of paisa and rupees. I gazed at the far end of the playground, at the raised walkway with its familiar red railings and the metal steps up and down. We used that walkway to and from our breaks. We played in that playground, Jean Duncan, Smita Shapurji, Pat and Veera and me. My extra lessons were after school hours, so all was quiet; no one else was around.

This was to help me get ready for England, because the term had nearly ended. Jan had finished school. We'd had six years of lengthy summers in Kodai. That was a long time in the lives of Jan and me, to absorb a place and embed it in our hearts. But now we were going to leave.

Leaving

In Madras the wooden boxes with metal edges seemed to have multiplied. Their heavy square shapes and pale wood smell filled the downstairs room. I understood that our leaving was definitely going to happen, but I could not understand why Ayah couldn't come too. Mum tried to explain. Ayah couldn't leave her family and friends and uproot from all her connections, and she wouldn't like the way of life in England. This is a difficult concept at any age – that the strength of your will and love cannot keep someone safe or happy or fulfil their every need.

The airport was small. It was a room with glass windows for people to see out to the planes, and a flat roof where they could stand and wave. Ayah came to the airport. We hugged and said goodbye and her face was all wet with tears. "My sweet lime my sugar lump my beauty face." Then Mum and Dad and Jan and I walked across the tarmac to the plane. Mum had my hand. I was crying.

Inside the plane, I sat beside the small round window. People had sorted their luggage and were settling down. I could see a lot of people on the flat roof, Ayah at the front of the crowd. I called out to her. I was sobbing, shouting so she could hear me through the window, across the space between us to the building where she stood. "Ayah, Ayah! I love you!"

"She can't hear you, darling," my mum said, and I turned to look at her and saw other people looking at me and smiling. What were they smiling for? How would I live without Ayah? How would she live without me?

Becoming number 60

Within two months of our return to England, I was getting ready to go to a convent boarding school in Surrey. I was nearly nine years old.

Jan tried to be encouraging. She talked about midnight feasts and pillow fights and the mischief I could get up to and all the fun I would have. I tried very hard to believe her. We had hardly unpacked our India boxes when we had to start packing my case. We bought my new school uniform, including new pants and vests, and a long list of things the school said I would need. Mum had rolls of narrow ribbon with 'No. 60' written on them. She sewed that number on to every item of clothing, on to everything I possessed.

But my dreams were still set in India, with India streets and India sounds and the sight of Ayah's face. Blue airmail letters from Ayah arrived every week with her address neatly written on the back. It wasn't

Khader Nawaz Khan Road any more; she had found work with an Indian family with two small children to look after. Ayah wrote to Mum and Jan, and a separate piece to me. My beauty face my sweet lime. Be a good girl for Mummy. I wrote back to her in my best, most careful writing. I told her oh Ayah I miss you and I sent her all my love. Ayah changed jobs a few times over the following years, and sometimes she had no employment. Things would have been very hard. I know my parents sent help, and I hope it made some difference, even if only small.

Through a few helpful twists of fate, we were able to move straight into a flat in Osterley, down the road from Dad's sister, my Aunty Peggy, and Uncle Arthur and their children, Rob and Bren. Our families had always been close, but now the Foxes became an integral part of our lives – especially my mum's, because Dad had to return to his work in India. The company agreed to fly him back a few times a year for breaks of a reasonable length. He had the easier option, I think – familiar work in a country he loved. He lived at the Madras Club in a small cottage they called The Hut. It's still there; I pass it every time we go. He had a taken-care-of lifestyle with a busy social life, but he also would have worked hard for long hours and was probably lonely at times. He wrote to Mum every day. She kept all his letters, which I now have, along with Jan's and mine. His letters were newsy and chatty. He talked to her as if they were together, about the people and happenings of his ordinary days, about his work and the politics of the country and the Club. "Honestly Moll, you won't believe what Desai is saying now. They want to put up the tax again and the businesses just can't afford it. Ridiculous. What do you think?"

Mum was left to adjust to life in England, with all the large and finer details that involved. Her priority was settling Jan – which meant helping her have the confidence to look for and start a job, to get on and off escalators and negotiate buses and trains, all new experiences and fraught with the possibility of falls. How excruciatingly nervous Jan must have been, and therefore how brilliantly brave. And how well, I think, Mum pitched her support and dealt with her own anxiety in order to lessen Jan's. She maintained that fine balance between cautious realism and optimistic belief as Jan went off for another interview, dressed just right and trying hard to control her arm and carefully manage her speech. I know it was an agony of worry for Mum, that Jan should not in any way or for any reason be made to feel unworthy or crushed. Finally, through a friend of the Foxes, she went for an interview with BOAC and was offered the job. She happily went off to Heathrow Airport on public transport every day. She made good friends there, and they all went out together and had evenings 'up in town'. Through a friend from her Kodai days, Liz, with whom I'm still in touch, she joined the Arthur Murray School of Dancing in central London. She couldn't do all the dances but was fine at the waltz and not too bad at the rumba and she let me help her practise her steps in the living room. While she was at Arthur Murray, Jan met Geoff, and she married him a few years later.

I could have been a day girl at a local school but, as Mum later explained, they thought it best for me to board from the start. They knew she would eventually be joining Dad in India, once Jan was established and settled enough to be left. I would then need to be in a boarding school, so they thought it best for me to go there from the beginning, rather than changing and having to get used to somewhere new later on. The company had already agreed to fly me back and forth for all holidays for as long as Mum was there. I do understand their thinking and I know the use of boarding schools for families abroad was not at all unusual at that time. But that second separation, so hot on the tail of losing Ayah, and the drastic contrast of place was unsettling, to say the least. We talked about this years later. I know Mum suffered at the thought of my struggles, but she hung on to the belief that this was the best thing to do.

I was No. 60, and I was in blue dorm. Two rows of child-sized, metal-framed beds – perhaps fifteen on each side – faced each other across a long and narrow room. Near each bed was a small chest of drawers and a cupboard. This was our cubicle, the only space in all the school, open and totally unprivate, that we could call our own. Sister Pauline was in charge of blue dorm. She had a cubicle only slightly bigger than ours with a thin partition around it. The walls of the partition didn't reach up to the ceiling, so in the night we could hear each other move. Sister Pauline had had polio as a child; she walked with a limp and had trouble using one arm. I thought this might give her a similar personality to Jan's – warm and funny and wanting to look after me – but I found that wasn't the case. She was very pale and very strict and always called me Frances. "Back in your cubicle, Frances. Quickly. It's time for lights out."

I cannot imagine how we small children got used to a building that size. How did we know where we were supposed to be or how to get there? It was an enormous old building with new bits added on. Passageways and corridors went on for miles and the hundreds of doors were always kept closed and you opened them with trepidation. Was this out of bounds or was everyone in there, waiting?

A walkway went along the front of some classrooms, past Mother Jo's office and on down a corridor to the dining hall. The wall we walked along was painted in a pinky-beige high gloss. It was dimpled and bumpy, and it formed a low ledge where it stuck out. That was where the incoming letters were placed, in class order. After lessons, at about four o'clock, we trooped along for bread and jam and tea. As we passed the pile of letters, we were allowed to look through to see whether there was one for us. I always neared that shelf with almost unbearable longing. To see my mum's writing, more familiar than my own face, was like having her present and near me. Her absence overwhelmed me. On one occasion I stood empty-handed, rooted to the spot and crying. Mother Jo must have been passing, and she called me into her office. She showed me warmth, and I know she understood the tsunami of loneliness that I was struggling to withstand. I sat on her lap and she held me while I cried. Not long after that, she wrote to Mum, suggesting I become a weekly boarder; she said it seemed a shame for Mum not to see more of me while she could. I didn't become a weekly boarder. Mum didn't drive, so in those early days, before I was old enough to be put on a train, she relied on Uncle Arthur. It would have been a lot to ask him to take me home and bring me back to school every weekend, so perhaps it was as simple as that?

At weekends we went in groups for what seemed like endless walks through fields and bracken. The bracken smelt of horses and all the colours were shades of brown or green – flat colours, subdued and chilly and damp. We gathered in clusters around radiators in the gym. I had no affinity to horses but volunteered to help in the stables just to vary the routine. The only absolute solitude was at night-time, alone in the dark in bed. I consciously saved up my thoughts till then so I could examine them in peace, uninterrupted, turn them over and think about them thoroughly in the quiet space of my mind. I still require good chunks of solitude at reasonable intervals in order to process and think.

We had half-term in the middle of term and a weekend out each side. Sometimes we were allowed an extra day out on a Sunday. A few weeks after I started at the school, Aunty Peggy and Uncle Arthur brought Mum and they took me out to a local fair. I cried from the minute I saw Mum until long after they had driven away. I begged her not to take me back to the school. I pleaded and pleaded for her to take me home. But they did take me back to the school. I have the letters I wrote during those early months.

"Dear Mummy. Please take me out. Please I miss you a lot. Please be at the school on Friday at 4 ok (o'clock) to take me out this Friday I will come back on Sunday at 5 ok. Please be here. Please."

"Ho (oh) I do miss you. PLEASE tell me how many days till I see you. Please mummy. I miss you."

After several years at the school, my spelling improves, but I am still obsessed by timing.

"The train arrives at Waterloo at 4.05 o'clock. That's 4 dot oh five. Please say you will be there please don't be late please be there at 4.05."

A Weekend Out

Back at home, Jan and I shared a room. Jan had it to herself a lot of the time, so all her things were on the dressing table – all her potions and perfumes, which she loved. I slept in my own single bed and adored it being just me and Jan and Mum. Often it was just me and Mum, as Jan was out with friends. The relief of being home. The joy. Friday night was the best as I still had all Saturday to come. We had something special for supper, perhaps sausages and mash and gravy, and Mum and I talked and watched television.

On Saturdays we met up with Aunty Peggy and Bren and went ice-skating at Richmond ice rink. We did this for years, right up to the point when Bren and I were far more interested in the boys than the skating. And we went to the Foxes' house, where Bren and I sat on their air raid shelter and sang songs. We did an excellent version of 'I've Told Every Little Star'. I did the 'dum di dum' bit and she sang the actual words, as she could sing in tune. We practised it hundreds and hundreds of times till we got the harmony and timing spot on. We also wrote and performed our own plays in Green Door Theatre (her garage doors were green). Later we started the Hayley Mills Fan Club, of which Bren and I were the only members. We paid weekly subs and took ourselves off for club outings. One of them was to Kew Gardens. And we had pet mice and a tortoise and silkworms and we did bob-a-job jobs for neighbours when it wasn't bob-a-job week.

By the Saturday evening of these weekends the dread was faintly lurking, but I tried not to let it roll in. I enjoyed our evenings together. Then our Sunday came. We watched an afternoon film and Mum bought us a Crunchie each. We took tiny tiny bites so we could make it last. I had a sickly feeling in my stomach. A slightly quivery chill.

Uncle Arthur and Aunty Peggy would come in the car to take me back to school. I had to be back by 5.00 p.m., so I think we left at four. My case was ready by the front door, and all through the afternoon I pictured it there and where it would be going. I had to change out of my home clothes and into uniform before we left, and even though it was washed and clean it still smelt strongly of school. Sometimes we drove in darkness. I sat in the back of the car with Mum and I could hear them chatting. I would look out of the window. A low-key nausea, an almost audible hum of dread. We stopped at the same shop every time, about twenty minutes from the school, where we bought my 'tuck' and Mum bought Uncle Arthur twenty Embassy cigarettes. I chose penny chews and arrows and sherbet dips and bull's eyes – sad sweets which I nursed on my lap as the journey got shorter and shorter.

Things did get better. I settled down and made good friends and we got up to no good together. My best friend was Lynne, who had also started there when very young. I realise now that separation from someone you feel loved by is probably easier to withstand than feeling uncared for in the first place. The unhappiness from one situation can seep into another, and I think that her existing unhappiness gave Lynne a perspective very different from my own. She remembers the school as horrendously cruel and barbaric. I remember it as an institution that was not warm and cosy but was not unduly harsh. Lynne has worked harder than anyone I know to understand and manage the adult ramifications of her earlier years. And she has succeeded. She is caring, creative and generous-hearted. She is my oldest friend.

Some people came to the school to enliven our interest in books. I wonder who they were and where they came from – perhaps some new educational initiative or something to do with libraries? We had a whole afternoon to browse through books and these people were there to make suggestions or tell us about the writers and the writing. The people who came were perfect for their task. They introduced me to the Liverpool poets, and I discovered Edwin Brock. I thought his *Five Ways to Kill a Man* was stunning; I still do. While I smiled at some of the jaunty Roger McGough poems, I was also drawn to the macabre or sad or disturbing. To know my complicated, sometimes sorrowful, feelings were not uncharted territory was a brilliant revelation and such a comfort to me. After their visit I felt I could be more open about my love of reading and also my need to write.

Riverview

Dad came back to England, supposedly to stay. He had to work in the Midlands so we had another move, away from Osterley to Barnt Green in Worcestershire. Jan and Geoff got married shortly before the move and not long after it Dad was asked to go back to Madras again, just for a year. This time, Mum would go with him.

I was thirteen by now and an adolescent mix of overconfidence and insecurity. My main interests were boys, clothes, make-up and music. I was also interested in books – mainly sad ones – and poetry and grappling with the meaning of life. One of my favourite books was *The Death of the Heart* by Elizabeth Bowen. I keep meaning to re-read it. I wonder what I would make of it now.

Mum was going back to Madras for a year on the understanding that I would fly out for all three school holidays. For half-terms and weekends out I would stay with Jan and Geoff. I also stayed with them for a few days at the beginning and end of each trip so they could help me with shopping and packing and get me on and off flights.

The first trip out was timed with my Easter holiday and the three of us – mum, dad and me – flew out together. They were sad to be leaving Jan and I'm sure she was anxious about them going, especially Mum; it was probably a tearful farewell. But Jan had her own home by then, and her life with Geoff, and she seemed happy and settled.

Our original flight was cancelled due to an Air India strike, so we ended up having five days' holiday in Beirut. Dad's cousin, who he hadn't seen for more than a decade, worked for Middle East Airlines and lived in Beirut, so we stayed in his apartment and he did an excellent job of showing us around. I still have a chunk of turquoise that we bought in one of the markets and a harem ring of Mum's. It was a beautiful city, yellowy-gold and clean and neat and tidy with modern boulevards and narrow lanes. You could stand in one spot and see the sea, the busy streets and the mountains. Not many years later, that city was ruins and rubble – I saw it every night on the news – and now it's in ruins again. Apart from Beirut, I have never seen the before as well as the after of a city destroyed by war. It helps me realise that the distraught, dust-covered people scrabbling in broken buildings really did lead normal lives on ordered streets with shops and cared-for homes. The volume of images of utter destruction sometimes make it hard to envisage there has ever been life before war.

We landed in Madras and happiness was the blast of heat as we got to the door of the plane. We were driven to the Madras Club, where we would stay for a couple of days as the house we would be living in wasn't ready. We drove through the gate and I saw the building and grounds, I heard the crows and caught a waft of the river.

Our rooms were at the top of some outside stairs, and on our first afternoon we had a call in the room to say there was someone to see us. I opened the door and looked down the steps. There was Ayah! Our letters had now almost fizzled out but she had heard on the grapevine that we were back. At times I could be a difficult and haughty teenager, but I flew down the steps and into her enormous cuddle. "My beauty face. My little sweet lime so big now!" She was shorter than me by then, but she smelt the same and felt the same and I was so happy to see her. We didn't need an ayah as I would hardly be there, but nevertheless she stayed with us for the full year

Mum was there.

The house we moved into was called Riverview. It was just opposite the Club, and the river it viewed was the Adyar. The river was generally an uninviting flat matt brown where buffaloes still swam and wallowed and boats occasionally glided by. It breathed out a gentle smell of sewage, which on some days you hardly noticed – a warm India smell, familiar and just as welcomed by me as the perfume of flowers or food or the muddled-up odours of a busy market or street. A casuarina wood edged the banks near our house, and occasional palms jutted into the sky on their thin but definite trunks. I loved their firm outline against a dark night sky or perfect daytime blue. I loved the view from the upstairs veranda of the Club's dome in the distance and the foreground of river and trees. I loved the incessant crows by day and all the sounds at night. The high-pitched noisy crickets. In the evenings the moon shone on the river and coloured it silver and gold. I loved the no-nonsense rain or heat – never drizzle. I loved India, unequivocal and so emphatic, where nothing was in between.

There were no other houses nearby, but one was being built not far away and I liked to watch the process. I watched the women as they placed two bricks side by side on their flat turbaned heads and repeated with two more bricks until their arms couldn't reach any higher. Then they walked with their load – straight-backed, erect, head unmoving – towards a ladder which they climbed. At the top of the ladder they unloaded their bricks two at a time for the men at the top to use.

There was a track from the main road to the house which a car could bump along. Small thatched huts lined the track, and chickens and dogs and children wandered about. A car was very unusual. Most people just ignored it but sometimes the children waved. The track ended near our house; it fizzled out into a pale, dusty path and spiky grass which only pedestrians and their animals could use. There were scorpions in the grass and along the edge of the river. Ayah said we must be very careful when walking. There were gulmohar trees with bright orange flowers, and creamy pale frangipani. Cerise and mauve bougainvillea climbed up the front of our house, and pots of lush plants were arranged around a pool – kidney shaped and blue, it was too small for actual swimming. When we arrived, it was the hottest time of the year, but everything was in flower. The colours were deep and strong. Every so often the mali found a cobra behind the pots in the garden and a cobra catcher had to be called in. He received a fee for every snake he caught, and on one occasion he showed us three, carefully, one at a time. Dad said it was probably the same snake, but we weren't in a position to quibble.

From my bathroom window I could watch people walk across the scrubland. They came from a village I couldn't see, along the path to the ferry boat just outside our house. Some people became used to seeing me and waved back to me as they walked past. The ferry was a small boat made to carry a handful of people, but it was usually crammed with dozens. It went to and from the other, busier side, carrying people to work or to shop or perhaps to visit their family. It had a very precarious wobble.

That first holiday was a quiet one for me. Not many people my age were flown out for the Easter break; mainly they came for the longer summer holiday. I went swimming at the Gymkhana Club, as wonderful as before, and I talked to the few other teenagers who were there. They were already looking forward to the summer when there would be lots of young people and parties and romances. The girls described the boys in detail, and who was likely to be with whom. And the boys did vice versa. They mentioned someone called Keith who they said was a bit of an outsider. Of course, he was the one I thought I'd like the best.

I went shopping with mum in Spencer's, where

she could buy her Yardley make-up. She used their vanishing cream and loose powder. The cream had a delicious smell and was orangey-pink and shiny. It came in a white porcelain jar with a dusky-pink screw top that had a small bee embossed in the centre. Spencer's also sold swimming costumes. They hung loosely on models raised high in the middle of the shop. They made you not wish to buy one. And they sold Nestlé's chocolate Brazil nuts in tall oval tins with flat lids. When we got home we prised the lids off using coins. The chocolates always looked dusty and patchy white but tasted as chocolate should. Spencer's had a tearoom at the front. It was air-conditioned, cool and perfumed, and always felt like a treat. Mum would have a cup of tea and I had a chocolate milkshake while we waited for our driver to arrive. The red-brick building of Spencer's was a landmark of Madras. There were much grander buildings, like the law courts and the museum and Fort St George, all of which are still there, but sadly Spencer's has gone. There is now an uninteresting high-rise building called Spencer Plaza with small forlorn-looking shops which are usually empty but somehow continue to survive.

On Sundays we went to film shows at the Club. Chairs were set out in rows on the side veranda and we all sat facing the screen with the whirring projector behind us. We tried not to sit with our parents. All the adults smoked and bearers brought drinks on trays and bowls of nuts and kept changing ashtrays for fresh ones. People dressed up for the film show and the Indian women looked gorgeous in silk saris in strong colours and their jewellery in glittering gold. European clothes, however lovely, lacked lustre by their side.

The summer holidays were everything I had hoped – so many people my age and a little older. It seemed to be endless get-togethers and parties, music and dancing and romance. I did meet Keith that summer. He wore white hipsters and a black string T-shirt and he smelt of fresh sweat and soap. We danced together at parties, me up against him, really close. He was tall and solid and I'd never been that close to a boy before. He had a Japanese girlfriend who wore wispy outfits on the beach. She had straight black hair and a lot of dark make-up on her eyes, and the sight of her made me feel very young and still the shape of a child. But Keith seemed to like me, and when we were back in England we wrote to each other from our respective schools. A few years later, when I was sixteen, he became my proper boyfriend. He stayed at our house for Christmas a few times, and I went to stay with his family. He gave me a small garnet ring and asked me to marry him when I was seventeen. I said no because I was too young, and we stopped seeing each other then. It was sad. He was a good person to have had as a first boyfriend.

I missed the big cyclone in November that year but felt I had been there from the stories Mum told me about it. Bloated black clouds appeared in the sky and it rained and rained for days. The river had waves and rushed by at frightening speed – and then flooded. It sloshed into the house like milky coffee and snakes slithered under the doors. Apparently there were fish on a ledge outside my upstairs bedroom. Wind roared and trees and wires came down and electricity went out. No lights no fridge no air conditioning. Mosquitoes were out in hordes, and Mum and Dad lay like corpses, wound in white sheets with incense burning around them, trying not to be eaten alive. After some days, when the water had subsided and the wind had quietened down, they went out to get supplies. It rained in their short absence and the river rose again. They had to leave the car at the end of the track and walk through thigh-high water. Mum wore Dad's trousers for some small protection, so he was in his underpants and shoes. They wondered if scorpions could swim. Several snakes swam past them and they used torchlight and sticks to try to scare them away. But despite all the fear and damage and excitement it caused them, they still had their home intact. The huts along the river and all over the coast of Tamil Nadu were dissolved and destroyed by the cyclone. Thousands of people who already had very little now had nothing at all. And the government did little to help.

Not long after the cyclone, I flew out for the Christmas holiday, the last one of that year's stint. For all I knew, I would be looking my last on India. The cyclone damage was strewn all around and the huts along our track were now just bits of thatch, small piles of stone and some rubble. Some were half-rebuilt as hope and habit triumphed. I looked from my bathroom window and wondered about the people from the village I couldn't see. People no longer walked back and forth to the ferry from that direction. Around 800,000 people had been made homeless; the newspapers said that dozens were killed, but it was far more likely to have been many, many hundreds. People from the unseen village were probably among them. Ayah's home was OK, and so were all her family.

There must have been Christmas parties but strangely I don't recall them. I only remember a quiet and subdued few weeks. A pall of disaster hung over the city as it tried to get back on its feet. The disparity of wealth and lifestyle still goes on and on.

Mum came to Bombay[13] with me to put me on my flight back to England. There were no direct flights in those days. I said my second and final goodbye to Ayah when she came to the airport in Madras to see us off. With Ayah a part of me was always eight years old, and I hugged her tight and cried. It was the last time I would see her. I looked for her when I next set foot in Chennai but the address and even the area no longer exists as it was. But really it doesn't matter. All these decades later, Ayah stays clear and strong. Eight years old is my 'regress to' age in times of serious trouble. I become that age and replicate the sensations of separation and the early months at the Surrey school when emotions felt too big too strong too awful to withstand. Most people have a default age, I think.

Mum and Dad left India together the following spring, in time for my Easter holiday. They were returning to Barnt Green, and shortly after they got back to England I changed school to one nearer them, where I was a weekly boarder. Lynne and I had been expelled from the convent. We went out of bounds once too often and then were caught smoking in green dorm bathroom when we were supposed to be elsewhere writing lines. Mother Jo

---
13 now Mumbai.

later wrote to Mum saying that on reflection she'd be happy to welcome me back. I think Mother Jo quite liked me, and I still have that letter. But it was too late by then and anyway it was more convenient for me to be near Barnt Green.

Part Two:
The Messy Middle

Decisions

Nearly twenty years later, in 1986, I had been living in Milan for seven years and now was about to leave. I was teaching English as a Foreign Language (TEFL) and had friends who I still know today.

There is a lot of humour in TEFL, and Norman and I still set ourselves giggling when we remember those teaching days. Norman and his husband Aldo now live in Rome, where I've visited them many times over the past forty years. They have met people important to me and have always made them feel welcome. Even people who are now in my past ask about NormanNaldo. They remember them in the car; Aldo is always behind the wheel and Norman always directs.

"Go right, Aldo, RIGHT! Why did you go left?"

"But Norman, look at that sign." They drive each other mad.

I went with Patrick to their wedding in 2017. It was in an ancient church near the enormous Circus Maximus in Rome, where the chariot races took place, and then at a restaurant on the Appian Way in open air and drenched in leafy sunlight. It was the happiest and easiest wedding I have ever been to. Italy is so good at pleasing all the senses, and Norman and Aldo made absolutely sure that it did.

Mum, Dad and Jan came to Milan for several holidays and Christmases, and various friends including Lynne and Gill visited several times. Gill was someone I knew from my Suffolk days when I trained and worked in probation, before I went to Milan. We met on our course at what is now the University of Suffolk. Over the years Gill and I have shared, at times, a rather manic zest for life as well as some hefty onslaughts. She and Steve have lived in France for decades, but we visit and speak on the phone.

Also in Suffolk, I married Simon, with whom I had shared my dope-smoking hippy days. He had long hair and he played guitar and he did law at uni, which didn't suit him at all. I thought he was very bright and good-looking – and really, I think, so did he. Girls flirted with him, and he happily flirted back.

In those early days, when I was supposed to be doing A levels, I hung around with Simon and the first-year students with their dishevelled clothes and the formula for acid scrawled on their flares and Camus or Nietzsche or Sartre sticking out of a pocket. That's what you did at that time, and that's who you wanted to be seen to be reading. I read writers I might otherwise have taken years to find.

Simon and I went to Milan together, teaching English. We were good friends, and he was a good companion to explore the country with. We did it justice, travelling all over the place – holidays in Calabria, weekends in Verona and Venice, and lunch overlooking Lake Como. With our group of friends we rented a chalet in the snowy mountains of the Val d'Aosta in the winter. Needless to say, I was cautious on my skis and found it scary just getting the hang of the lifts. In the summer, with the same group of friends, we had a house in Liguria by the sea. It had a large terrace and bright red geraniums which we watered in the fresh evening sun. The deep, strong, warm plant smell of geraniums. Green shutters, ochre terrace, blue sea.

Milan was where my friend Nigel was ill with AIDS. He was flown back to England in a special hospital plane. When I last saw him he was in a wheelchair, with eyes the size of plates. He told me he was frightened. Looking back into his eyes, I was frightened too, that I didn't know how to help him. Not long after, he died at the Middlesex Hospital, with everyone masked and gowned.

Milan was where my longing to have a child was at its height, but it was where I didn't have one. This absence took on a life of its own and created life-changing choices. The cascade of choices I made. A death knell for me and Simon. After fourteen years together, since we had been virtually children, in Milan we parted ways. The mammoth decisions of that time still have strong ripples today.

I met D in Milan. Gentle philosopher, I Ching reader, guitar player and cook. He was my awakening. He helped me see myself through his eyes, valued beyond all words, and to know myself in an intense and different way. Mutual shock and the jiggling of atoms on my skin. I felt more alive on two hours' sleep than I ever had on eight. Decades later, long after we were apart, his wonderment still had the strength to sustain me, and there were times when I needed to use that strength. I conjured him clearly in my mind. We didn't end; we just stopped being together while we got on with our separate lives. He was the embodiment of Italy, which I loved. I loved its cities and lakes and mountains and sea. I loved the coffee and the food and the vino. The people. Its temperament suited me.

But another decision was brewing. I had known this would happen and that I would eventually leave.

I'll just have one more summer, one more Christmas, then I'll leave. I think there is a sense when living abroad of a line of no return. A make-your-mind-up time when you either stay in the foreign country and make it your permanent home or return to wherever you come from. Where can you picture yourself? Where is 'home'?

In 1985 I planned a trip in the hope it would act as a buffer zone, perhaps loosening ties between me and D and ultimately helping me decide. I would use the money from the sale of the Suffolk house with Simon. At that time I was teaching at a state school, so had long, paid holidays. I paid two months' rent up front and had everything in order so that D could either stay in the apartment or stay with his family at their home. His finances were always unstable, so I had to make sure all was sorted for when I returned.

I flew from Milan to London and had a few days with Mum and Dad before I set off for the trip. By this time they had moved to Surbiton, within easy reach of Heathrow. I was not going back to Chennai but would be starting in Delhi, so at least I would touch Indian soil.

The Trip

My flight was on the 24th June 1985. On the evening of the 23rd I was packed and ready and enjoying a drink with Mum and Dad while we watched the news on the tele. Suddenly we all sat up and really listened. Air India Flight 182 had blown up just off Ireland, killing everyone on board. There were 307 passengers and 22 crew, and 82 of the dead were children under thirteen. The flight was from Montreal via Heathrow and Delhi to Bombay. It was the same airline and route that I would be on the next day.

On 24th June I boarded my Air India flight from Heathrow to Delhi. Flight 182 was supposed to blow up on the tarmac at Heathrow Airport but was 1½ hours delayed in Montreal, so blew up in Irish airspace instead. Had it been on time, my crew and many of the passengers on my flight might have been on it when it exploded. As it was, the crew who died on Flight 182 were all known to, and friends of, my crew. I cannot imagine how they felt as they boarded the plane and still looked after us passengers through the flight. It was the deadliest act of aviation terrorism until the 9/11 attacks in 2001 and remains the worst terrorist attack in Canada's history. Sikh extremists were held responsible, but to my knowledge only one person has been convicted (in 2003), and many grieving families believe the catastrophe has never been fully investigated. It does seem strange that everyone knows about the Lockerbie disaster but I can't think of a single person who has even heard of Flight 182.

The flight was terrifying and turbulent but we landed in one piece, and I was met by Ritu and Harrish and their son Ashu. They were the family Dad did consultancy work for, and he stayed with them on his India stints. He had his own room in their house with his clothes still hanging in the wardrobe. It was his home from home. It was where he loved to be, and the people were the people he loved to be with. Really, he would happily have lived there if it hadn't been for Mum, Jan and me. He had been in India probably more on than off for forty years and I completely understood the sense of belonging he felt there.

I had Dad's room, which felt comfortable with his possessions. Next door was a small puja room with Hindu gods and garlands and offerings where Ritu prayed each day. Their son was very unwell with a rare disease which involved frequent blood transfusions, and she prayed and prayed for his health.

It was my first time in Delhi. Ritu and Harrish and all the different family members looked after me beautifully and showed me all the sights. One day we left early for Agra and I saw the Taj Mahal. It was exquisite and romantic – and it was also a Friday, free entrance day, so absolutely packed with people and the sun was so boiling hot I could feel my brains bubbling in my skull. That evening, we returned to Delhi and went to the son et lumière at the Red Fort. Various sections made me hang my head to be British, but these are the facts of history. No one threw stones as I left.

I spent time in the houses of extended family members, all of whom talked of Dad with such warmth and fondness that they almost had me in tears. He knew them well, their ailments and worries and aspirations and exasperations with their children, and they seemed to know about us. "He does worry about you, you know. He wants you to be happy," said Indu. She was one of the extended family, a lovely woman. In one of my letters I say how much I like her and that we spent hours chatting together "about life and all sorts of things".

We travelled in air-conditioned cars and ate lunch in hotels I'd never seen the like of before. Acres of immaculate marble flooring and rooms the size of a park. The food was delicious, as were the snacks we had at home and the mangoes I couldn't stop eating. We went to the Moti Mahal restaurant which Dad so highly recommended, and I had chicken butter masala. I could eat it all right now.

I was in Delhi for just five days, and I know that my stay was very privileged. Then I moved on with the rest of the trip, which was far more down to earth. I went to Bangkok and Ko Samui, Hong Kong, Japan and then the States. In Japan I met up with Simon, who was by that time working there.

I have the journals and letters I wrote throughout these travels. I could not have spent the money more wisely. I remember every moment of the journey – the flights and buses, the people, the hotels and huts and hostels, the sights, the food, the scary bits, the joy, the sense of pleasure that I had sorted every move and every aspect and that it had all worked out so wonderfully and perfectly well. I loved travelling on my own. I could be super-organised or loose with arrangements as and when I wanted. There were always other travellers to be with if I chose, and I met and spent time with many people in many different ways. But I also loved the undiluted strength of experiencing something on my own. I didn't need to discuss it or share it at that moment. Its intensity felt unspoilt. Many people's experiences are enhanced by being able to share them, and I can understand that; often, now, I feel that way too. But on that trip the combination of solitude and company was absolutely perfect for me.

I flew from Tokyo to Los Angeles by Japan Airlines. By grim and extraordinary coincidence, the previous day, August 12th, JAL Flight 123 had suffered structural failure and crashed after flying with minimal control for thirty-two minutes, giving passengers time to write notes to loved ones. It had a high-density seating configuration and carried 15 crew and 509 passengers. There were four survivors. For some reason a crew member on our plane decided to give us this information halfway through our flight. Luckily for me you could still smoke on flights then, so I expect I lit up and swiftly downed a large brandy and ginger ale.

Back to England

In 1986 I left Italy and returned to England. I left by train as I could take more luggage, and I remember every inch of the way. I have never returned to Milan. The seven years I was there include some of the happiest and saddest times of my life, the brightest and darkest threads. Its intensity hasn't waned, and I wouldn't want it to. But those years are another story.

Leaving Milan might have been an extraordinary decision, but probably it was right. Dad had started having mini-strokes and Mum was recovering from a massive bowel cancer operation. She was also very forgetful. I lived with them in their Surbiton flat a stone's throw from the river, and Jan was living nearby.

I started an English language school in Kingston upon Thames. I dealt with every aspect of the school, constructing and selling and providing the courses. I taught people from Japanese companies and Italians from my contacts in Milan. At one time I needed eight teachers. Luckily the school was successful, and I worked very hard.

Dad's condition got worse and in December 1986 he went into Kingston Hospital. At least we had had some time together, walking to the shops or the local pub while his legs were still able to function. I talked to him about the school and once I asked him, "Should I go back to Italy, do you think?" He gave me an emphatic "No" but sometimes his words came out all wrong, so I wasn't sure of his answer. My proud, funny, dignified and always enthusiastic dad now couldn't move or speak. They gave him a card with pictures on it that he could point to when he needed to wee. At Christmas they tied tinsel to his bed and a small choir sang 'Silent Night'. There was a tear on his face. I cannot bear that carol. On 18th February 1987, he died. Mum went downhill after that, although she tried to hang on by a thread. Every morning I felt the thud of realisation that he'd gone – and after my own awakening, I would then hear Mum as she woke and understood. I sat beside her with my arms around her while she cried. There was absolutely nothing to say.

Walking along the river with Geoff one day, we

saw a narrowboat for sale at Thames Ditton. I needed a place of my own, but because of my self-employment I couldn't get a mortgage, and I'd had enough of renting in Milan. With money left from the Suffolk house and a small 'advance' from Mum, I bought the boat.[14] It was wonderfully equipped and comfortable. Jane, who I knew from college in Suffolk, was a very boaty person, and still is. She has had thousands of miles of nautical adventures and doesn't intend to stop. She and her husband, Pete, taught me three-point turns on the Thames and the people at the marina showed me what I needed to know. The boat was forty feet long and ten feet wide and I managed to manoeuvre it single-handed. Amazing what you do if you have to.

I kept working hard, for long hours. A wine bar in Kingston became my local as I called in on my way home. I met people there and spent time with them at weekends. Everything seemed to include drinking. Unlike in Italy, where food is always involved, this was drinking for drinking's sake. I consumed too much wine and had too many liaisons. Life felt unsettled and lonely. I missed Milan and Dad and D. I think I looked like a sitting duck – and

---

14 The boat was called *Winchester*, named for the pub in the TV series *Minder*. Its previous owner, and the person who'd had it built, was the actor Glyn Edwards, who (among other leading roles) played the part of the pub's landlord.

soon someone spotted me. A muddled mix of need and hope led to peculiar decisions and I packed up the school and sold the boat and moved to live with him. One of my not so good choices.

Several months later Gill and Steve came to get me. They picked me up from his house when he was out and took me back to theirs, miles away in Yorkshire. I stayed with them for weeks and weeks until my head had settled and I started work and could set up home on my own. I still thank them, Gill and Steve.

Laws and attitudes, police response and support can help protect women, but ultimately the issue is: what can be done to change the behaviour itself? What creates that version of masculinity, that misogynistic rage? Where does the paranoia come from, the relentless insecurity and fear? What is their history? Why is it mainly males? Many abusers have witnessed abuse or been on the receiving end. They may know and loathe the suffering it causes, but still they repeat the process. What extreme powerlessness creates that need for power? What drives that calculated madness to damage and punish or even kill the victim, and themselves?

Yorkshire

I got back into probation work and the minute I started a permanent job I bought a house of my own. I touched the walls and felt so safe and happy. I had my boxer puppy, Bif. I loved my house and my work and having Gill and Steve down the road. I met people through them and at work and got to know my neighbours. Mortgages were easy to get in those days, but interest rates were high. I had to count my pennies and do some clever juggling, but I had enough to survive. Probation was reasonably well paid.

Mum and Jan often visited. Jan and Geoff were divorced by then, but he brought them up and stayed; he and Jan were amicable enough for that to work out well. I was happy and settled. My darling Bif gave me all the love and the warmest of cuddles that any human could need. I really loved that boy.

About six months after moving into the house, I met T. He was doing a placement at our probation office. T is the funniest person I have ever known. His impersonations and observations were always spot-on and warm-hearted, with a perfect knack for accents and choice of his characters' words. He was never disparaging – neither of us liked that kind of humour – and he made many people smile. The most brilliant thing about T and me was that the ticklement was mutual; he found me hilarious too. We made up Bif songs in the car, and sometimes we laughed so much I had to pull over as I couldn't see to drive. Our wits, in both senses of the word, coincided.

We both loved our work and could happily discuss it for hours. We trusted each other's judgement. It was exacting work with serious decisions to be made. We dealt with high-risk people – some high-profile ones, too – and with others who were painfully vulnerable, trapped in addictions or low expectations and feeling they had no choice. There were always choices, but sometimes they were hard to locate. At weekends we brought home reports to write, to free ourselves up the following week to cope with our sky-high caseloads. We wrote in separate rooms and stayed quiet until we had both finished.

We began our Friday nights late with favourite food

and drink. With his glass of wine, T would consult the *Racing Post*. That was his absolute element, happily fraught with anticipation of the weekend races to come. We watched something simple on tele, – "Tonight, Matthew..." – and then danced our socks off into the night or talked our hearts out, putting our worlds to rights. His had not been easy and I felt his childhood almost as if it were mine. I could picture his house, the rooms, the streets and the people he'd had to run from. His intelligence and insight could not make it loosen its grip.

You can talk and talk and understand but still it can scupper your life and mess up your best intentions. We tried to hang on to all that was good about us, but in the end ourselves, our histories and losses and more complicated things won out. We probably did well to last ten years, although the final two were awful. Jan, Bif, T's dad, T's brother and then my mum all died. I think that nailed down our coffins.

Mum and Jan

I sat beside Mum in hospital. She was oblivious to where she was or why. We sat quietly side by side, holding hands, watching the ward go by. Mum was always delighted to see me, and when I left a room for a minute she was delighted again when I got back. I think the sight of my face helped her make sense of her world; she seemed to know that I knew who she was, so where she was didn't matter. Her happiness at seeing me nearly killed me. The thought of her being frightened if I wasn't there.

By now we had both stopped struggling – me to make her remember, and her to try not to forget. It made our lives much easier. She no longer searched for context, the panicky rummaging through her bag or home for clues as to what was going on. Years ago, when Dad was still alive, she had known it was starting to happen. At first it seemed her mind just skipped a beat, a fleeting unfamiliarity with a word or a face or a street. Frightening but fleeting, and you could almost explain it away. But without Dad the gaps became more gaping. No subtle prompts no conferring no ally to help cover her tracks. She was lonely and stranded without him and exhausted by the effort of trying to get by.

At the beginning she knew Dad was dead and that Jan lived nearby and that I was up in Yorkshire. She knew our numbers were at the top of a list by the phone. She knew Jan was ill and struggling. She knew her words could vanish mid-sentence and her intentions get lost mid-stream. She said her thoughts were like quick silver fish which darted away before she could reach to hold them. Words would not be spelt right and notes to herself just fizzled out before she could complete them. Time became jumbled and its contents emptied away. She had a physical sensation of feeling very tall with her head very far from her feet.

You cannot be seen to be losing your mind. It's undignified and embarrassing. Mum remained herself, still courteous and kind, a mirror image of what she thought she should be. She tried very hard to imitate herself exactly. There are so many threads to pull together to make a day a day. Now you wash, now you dress, now you cook and you eat. How did you used to do that? The outlines of functions were there but the details had rubbed away. The habit of processes would get her halfway through but then suddenly back away, leaving her baffled with a kettle in her hand, lost in a shop, riskily uncertain at the sight of raw meat in the fridge. She loved to read, so would open a book with all the anticipation of before. But the print would not connect into words; there was no continuity, no sense. Images on television were just images on television; there was no before or after, no thread or beginning or end.

Jan worked hard to help pull Mum's days together. She had dozens of phone calls and visited every day. Carers now came to help and friends phoned or occasionally called in. But the contact with friends started to dwindle, as it often does. It was tricky and unrewarding for them when Mum didn't know who they were.

It was now two years since Dad had died, and she was very lost and precarious. Jan was exhausted and getting ill from the strain of caring. So the decision was made that Mum would come and live with me. T and I had been together for several years, and he had moved in with me. Sometimes we lived together and sometimes, for short stints, we didn't. He understood that both Mum and Jan needed me to take over, and he said he was happy with the arrangement. I think he thought he'd have two women looking after him, but instead he lost part of me. It can't have been easy for him.

Mum said, "That would be lovely, darling!"

Jan and I went through all her precious possessions, including photos and letters, and carefully packed all she or we would want or need. The flat was packed up for us to sort some time later. We waved to Jan as we pulled away, Mum strapped in safe and happy and Jan relieved to have the space to try to gain some strength. This move did not feel dramatic. There was no momentous sense of this being the end of Mum having her own home. Her time there had now become almost entirely unhappy. So we sang songs on the journey up and chatted in a 'here and now' way. She wanted to hear again and again what the plan was, not so that she would remember but because she liked the plan.

Mum had met T several times, but still she kept calling him Simon. She had known me with Simon for fifteen years, so of course it made sense that T was obviously Simon. Sometimes things were very good between T and me, and sometimes they really weren't. For those brief times, on and off, we couldn't live together.

I went part-time and loved the days not working. Mum and I went on outings and we shopped together and cleaned the house and pottered around the garden. She deadheaded and watered, she peeled the vegetables and polished silver. She arranged flowers beautifully in a vase. All these things she did without thinking, as perfectly as before. Neighbours were happy to be vigilant and friends like Gill and Steve were, as always, thoughtful and willing to help. T's mum, Olwen, sometimes stayed and they sat holding hands on the sofa. We listened together to the Big Band sound and sang the songs and jived. Mum was a brilliant dancer.

Jan visited when possible and in between we had numerous calls each week. She liked to hear the stories.

The one where Mum had left the hairdresser's, unaccompanied, minutes before I had arrived to collect her. I was frantic. She could have wandered in any direction, completely unaware of how to get herself home. Anything could have happened – traffic, mugging, gangs of cruel people making fun. I ran back to the house in case she had found her way there. The phone was ringing. The woman had found my details in Mum's bag. They were having a nice cup of tea in the woman's lounge and a lovely chat about roses. The woman had found her looking lost and taken her into her home. I hugged her so hard when I collected Mum, and the next day we took her some roses.

The one where I returned from work to see a police car parked outside. I rushed in. T was looking helpless while being questioned, and Mum was looking on with a policewoman holding her hand. "Oh, hello darling!" She beamed at me to welcome me into this happy little gathering she'd arranged. She'd dialled 999 to tell the police she'd been abducted and didn't know where she was. The police had arrived just before T and were still considering whether or not he lived in that house and whether he should or should not be trusted. Bif sat watching from his chair, his 'well, I'm a good boy' look on his baffled boxer face. Mum had no clue who T was. Luckily I was there only minutes later, so could explain what I thought had happened. The police were understanding and Mum, oblivious to any drama, offered them a nice cup of tea and thanked them for popping in.

Jan loved these stories, and the sound of her giggling always made me laugh. But sometimes things just weren't funny.

I could return from work and find Mum looking lost. I would find her standing in the middle of the room as if she had been searching, trying to fathom her surroundings, where in the world she was. At work I worried and I worried as I rushed to get home. As far as I knew, she had never chosen to leave the house – but if she had, she would have been lost in seconds. Inside the house I made things as safe as possible. After a 3.00 a.m. flood from a filling bath, all plugs had been removed. The knobs were off the gas cooker and any matches were well beyond reach.

In some ways she was quite independent. I put toothpaste on her brush and she would brush her teeth. She would wash herself once safely in the shower, and dry herself if a towel was placed nearby. We chose her clothes together, only gentle nudging as she still had impeccable taste. But some processes defeated her completely, such as kettles. Without guidance and prompting she couldn't make a cup of tea. When I was at work, carers called in at intervals through the day. They prepared her food and checked that she was alright. But she wasn't alright. She had too many hours alone with the risk of harming herself.

A local residential home, Claremont, provided day care. It takes an enormous mind leap to picture your person there. Mum would not have chosen to spend whole days in the company of strangers, eating what she was given at a table with people she didn't know. She would feel compelled to be sociable. So exhausting to keep up for whole days.

Safety, happiness and aloneness were all difficult aspects to weigh.

Arrangements with carers, taxis, neighbours and friends were in place and for over a year they were steady. Sometimes a friend would stay with Mum while T and I went out, and a wonderful woman from a voluntary organisation sometimes came for the evening. They shared supper and pottered and watched TV, and then she would help Mum to bed. T and I would get home to a sparkling kitchen as the volunteer had thought she'd give herself something to do while Mum was safely asleep. Sometimes Jan and Geoff came to stay while T and I went away. T was not involved in the actual caring for Mum, and I tried very hard to divide myself between them. He wanted my time to be separate, and I wanted to create that space.

Time passed, and Claremont suggested respite – perhaps just a few days every couple of months? Jan and I agonised again, about how Mum would feel in a strange bed and room. I explained it to her: that I might go away for a little break and I'd know she was safe, which would stop me worrying. "That's a wonderful idea, darling. I like it there and I'd love you to have a break." She absolutely never tried to make me feel guilty. She was trusting and considerate of me, always amenable to any suggestion I made.

When I picked her up after that first respite period, she looked relaxed and cheerful, so I knew she had been OK. I always knew how things were in my absence from the residue of emotions which lingered. Her mood spoke volumes, and her demeanour was louder than words. Some restlessness, a tightness in her posture, an agitated stance or walk, bewilderment in her eyes, a defiant mouth, a subtly dishevelled look. Some roughness or impatience or uncaring gesture or brusque words would have left a trace, however faint, some sense of the hurt they caused. But I knew she was alright at Claremont. Mum seemed to cope and be more adaptable to the idea of Claremont than either Jan or me.

T and I looked forward to the regular respite, though usually we just stayed at home. I began to realise my constant alertness to Mum's needs. A constant tension that things might suddenly go wrong. A state of half-expectation all day at work and half-awake vigilance all night. At home, unless held by the company of another person, Mum followed me from room to room. I could hear her swift steps on the stairs and feel her waiting and wondering on the other side of the bathroom door. Her neediness and vulnerability were becoming an extension of me. Our edges were blurring and I wasn't always sure where she ended and I began.

At work they offered me back the other half of my

job. Cutbacks were fierce, and this was unlikely to happen again. Jan and I talked about a permanent move to Claremont. Just speaking of it made me cry; perhaps I was just tired, already at a low ebb. Jan thought I should take the job, and really so did I. But the process was so awful. My precious mum with all her life contained in one small room.

I talked to her about it. "Well, I think it would be rather nice – a place of my own just down the road from you. I don't want you worrying, darling."

Mum was self-funding because of the flat, but a social worker still had to be involved. He was good and not patronising to Mum or to me. He seemed to understand that the questions on the forms would feel most peculiarly alien, heartbreakingly practical and succinct.

Once Mum was there, I drove down to Surbiton and Jan and I met for a last weekend in the flat. We went through everything to be sold or given away or to be kept by Jan or me. It did not feel wrenching to drive away, as Mum hadn't been there for nearly two years while she'd been living with me. The flat was put on the market and luckily sold quickly.

Taking Mum to Claremont was one of the saddest journeys I have ever made. This was not respite. It felt like abandonment to a strange and unintimate world. All her clever choices, all the effort and plans and fine taste she had put into the making of her homes in England and far away. All her travels. All our moves as a family. All her life would now be there in rooms which were not her own. But she had a few pieces of her own furniture, some ornaments and books and photos and some pictures on the wall. She had her favourite possessions which she loved to tell me about. She had already written *From Pillar to Post*, and I had it typed up and gave a few copies to Claremont. Several people read it and loved it, so at least they knew something of her past, something of who she was.

Edwina was Mum's personal carer. She was Polish and a Catholic. She would chat with Mum while they tidied the room together, and Mum would fluff a pillow that Edwina had put a fresh cover on. I know she talked to Mum about her family and her home and her worries about her son. Edwina told me she liked talking to Mum because she always knew she would get a perfect response of concern or interest or fun. Mum's words could be astonishingly appropriate, uncannily spot on. On Sundays Edwina and her husband called to take Mum to Mass. Sometimes I went with them and then brought Mum home for lunch. In church, she knew her childhood prayers and hymns, the old unchanging ones. I stood beside her and listened to her sing. Faultless and in tune, she sang with an earnestness which made my heart ache. Mum always recognised Edwina – not who she was exactly, but as someone good who was comfortable to be with.

I used to dwell on how Mum spent her days and evenings and nights. I hated waving goodbye. There was a small upstairs balcony off a room that was used for daytime activities; it was always empty in the evenings when everyone was in other rooms. When I left, Mum would find her way to this balcony and would stand and wave as I got into my car. She watched as I pulled away. In my mirror I saw her stop smiling as she turned and walked back into the empty room. I worried and worried about her feeling sad or lost or alone. But often, when I arrived unannounced, I could see for myself how she spent her time. Sometimes sitting quietly but seeming contented on her own in her room. Or watching television in the lounge or with Edwina or another carer, dusting ornaments, or eating or sitting in the garden with other people. It became a quiet existence as exchanges of words were brief, no back and forth of conversation or lengthy ribbons of words.

Over time I felt that Mum was settled, but Jan was increasingly unwell. Jan had been a '*Hello* magazine' sort of person. She loved the gossip and always knew what was going on with some actress or politician

I'd never heard of. She was also an excellent listener and had been a Samaritan for years. Now she was barely mobile and was trapped in every sense. She over-ate and over-drank and was overwhelmed by unhappiness. I visited and phoned and wrote to doctors but I didn't know how to help. She was in and out of hospital and I was up and down the motorway as often as I could.

On 17th September 1996, Jan died. T and I were both with her. She was fifty-three, nine years older than me. After the funeral, T and I drove back up the motorway, and I knew I would have to tell Mum. It felt too crucial not to tell her.

For whole minutes she felt the horror of what I had said. She seemed to physically collapse into herself and kept repeating "Jan? My Jannie? Jan?" as though it was not possible for it to be true. I held her and we both cried. Sitting on her bed, my arms around her, minutes passed, until I could feel her sobbing subside. It became quieter and I could feel her understanding of the sobbing drifting away, leaving her under a dark shadow of sadness, a dreadful detached sadness, so strangely adrift from its source. Mum, with all this feeling, not knowing where it had come from. I left some hours later, with Edwina now by her side. Mum was subdued, with bewildered eyes, but I don't think she remembered

Jan was dead.

I didn't cope very well with the loss of Jan. The only other keeper of memories of our childhoods, our family, my life. But I know there are fates worse than death and storms we really cannot weather, and I would not have wished that for her. Mum often asked about Jan and Dad. "It seems ages since I've seen them. Dad working away, I suppose?" She would wonder how Jan was doing and I'd say she was fine and sent her love. And I liked to believe this was true.

Over the years I had a number of scares with Mum. A call from Claremont to say they had called an ambulance and they thought it might be her heart. It wasn't, but I would drive to the hospital preparing myself for the worst. I had the resus discussion with twelve-year-old doctors, saying I probably wouldn't want them to jump up and down. One year we even had Last Rites, for which I was not ready. When I was ten, I used to pray my parents would not die until I was thirteen. I thought by then I'd be old enough to bear to live without them. At thirteen I wanted them to wait till I was at least twenty-one, then until I was married, then till I had recovered from the divorce. I wanted them to see me happy. I'm not sure we are ever really ready, but I tried to look as though I was.

I was always anxious when Mum was in hospital,

because I knew she wasn't safe. Once I found her two miles of corridor away from her ward, sitting on a bench outside the endoscopy department, her raincoat over her nightie. When would they have noticed she had gone? And cartons of drink unopened by her bed, impossible for her to fathom how to open. She must drink fluids, they had said. She was prodded for veins and lifted by bruising hands under her fragile arms. She looked so bemused and baffled.

Mum was in A&E four times. Twice I burst through the curtains to find her all smiles on a trolley. "Oh, darling! What are you doing here?" And there were a few day visits. One was an X-ray involving drinking pints of water and then trying not to wee. In the waiting area people were in tears of distress as they hung on to bursting bladders. A woman wept at the effort and an elderly man stood at the door of the toilets, drenched, in an agony of mortification. My mum miraculously held on. X-ray all clear. Wrung out and wretched with worry, I walked with her back to the car. "Well, it's been a lovely day hasn't it, darling!" Smiling and happy. We were in the car together, so we must have been somewhere nice.

She was always alert to happenings around her and willing to be pleased and to giggle. I told her the stories I knew would make her smile. I had a repertoire of ancient, familiar stories I told again and again which she never tired of hearing and which we both knew off by heart. "That time you and Dad went camping and locked the car keys in the car!" "And we were in our pyjamas with all our clothes in the car!" She threw her head back and caught my eye, full of life and laughter. Some of these memories were entirely Mum's but were so familiar that I felt as if they were mine.

Her memory had gone but it hadn't. Layer upon layer was still present, and the lower strata were astonishingly intact. Sometimes they just needed unearthing. We looked through photos in muted black and white and shades of cream and some with a shadow of colour. She recognised dresses she wore and decisively remembered the colours. Photos with Dad, heads close, skin touching, on a beach, outside houses, in their gear on his Enfield bike. The oldest album is my favourite. It has a thick brown paper cover with the word 'Snapshots' printed in a jaunty, wavy way in black letters overwritten in turquoise-green felt-tip. The pages are nearly as thick as the cover, except at the edges, where years of turning have made them soft and thin. My dad's neat handwriting guides us through those years. 'Oakhanger 1936. Our Honeymoon.' There are three photos in sequence of the rise, the height and the fall of a wave. 'Three stages of a wave breaking. Trebarwith Strand. 1938.' There are dozens of photos of my mum on her own or of Dad or of the two of them together where he notes the place, not the person. Only when they appear with other people are they named. 'Gilbert, Molly and self.'

Mum went into hospital in the first week of the new millennium. She died on the 7th of January. I had been with her all the previous days but Gill and Steve had come to the hospital the evening before, with T, and for a muddle of reasons I was keen to leave and have time with them before going home to sleep. I instigated our leaving. I don't know what was expected, but no one said I should stay. I feel I should have known. Mum died on her own in the early hours of the morning. I can't change that. I have to believe that she was asleep and OK.

Part Three:
The End

India, 2002

After all the deaths and the tensions between me and T, I decided to return to India, to go back to what was now Chennai, for the first time since I was thirteen. It was blatant nostalgia, a wish to touch my past and feel connected to the people who had been in it. I would be away for three weeks. I drove from Yorkshire to Geoff in Surbiton, and he took me and picked me up from Heathrow. I phoned T from Geoff's the night before I left. He was encouraging and loving and tearful. That was the T I would miss.

The coincidences and luck associated with the trip were seriously uncanny, and I truly felt they were the work of Jan and Mum and Dad, who were now my precious ghosts. Every day in Chennai I was astounded by the depth of familiarity around me, all the more astonishing given the amount of change that had taken place. Strangers wanted to help me; they pored over my old photos and discussed possibilities with other strangers on the street. From my 1950s photo a passer-by recognised the house on Khader Nawaz Khan Road, now hidden behind and between other buildings, and he guided me to the back of an office from where – I saw our house! It was luck that the owner was there on that particular day. He was overseeing the process of turning the downstairs into a Punjabi restaurant. I knew immediately that he understood my quest and even seemed to share the wash of emotions. He let me walk around every inch of the house and let me video as I wanted. He said I could go back any time to just sit quietly and think.

And I sat in the unchanged church I used to go to with Ayah. I had letters written by her with her address on the back. They were written nearly forty years earlier, but I went to the Thousand Lights area clutching photos of Ayah and her address at that time. People tried to help – they wanted me to find her or perhaps her daughter – but unfortunately to no avail. I walked around the dusty grounds of Church Park School with its perilously shiny red floor. I had tea and cake with Sister Basil who used to be up in Kodai. We called her 'Sister Daddy' because she had Dad's name. A very strange thing happened to do with Sister Basil. Before I left England, I had mailed the main India site for Presentation Convent to try to get a contact number for Sister Basil. I wrote 'to whom it concerns' as I didn't have a name. I received a mail back with an email address for Sister Basil, saying they were sure she would be pleased to hear from me. It ended "God bless you. From Sister Molly." Sisters Basil and Molly! That still makes my hair stand on end.

On the same day as the house and church and school, I passed a hoarding on a roundabout which said "T I Cycles, Murugappa Group" – the company Dad had worked for, with the factories he had set up. He and Mum had been friends with the Murugappa family, so that name was very familiar and it seemed so strange to see it there, as if it were waving to me.

I went to the Gymkhana Club with its blue-tinged water and what looked like the same diving board and slide as when I was thirteen years old. And then to the Madras Club. Through the gates and into a time warp of bright white buildings and beautiful leafy green. The grounds, the buildings, the trees, the verandas and the play area at the side were all as I remembered. The sound of the air was the same, it had a softness to it, muffled despite the crows. I had arranged the visit before I left England and I was made so welcome by everyone I met. Ramesh Lulla met me and showed me around. He said I should move from my hotel and stay at the Club, so I arranged to do that on my return from another trip I had planned. I visited the Boat Club where I had danced with Keith. We drove over the bridge and down a track and eventually found Riverview. There were large gated houses along the track, and Riverview looked much grander than I had remembered.

I had planned a trip which included some retracing of steps from my mum's 1966/7 diary. Thyagu (pronounced 'T R goo') would be my driver for the full ten days away, and he drove me for the rest of the holiday. Thyagu was in his late twenties, immaculately turned out with his ironed shirts and oiled and quiffed black hair. He said he wanted to be an actor and he told me about his family; he lived with his grandmother and sisters as his father had run off and his mother had died many years before. Someone he knew had died by self-immolation. Thyagu was a good and careful driver. On our way back to the city from wherever we had been, he would always say, as we set off in the car, "Now we go stately to Chennai." When I am driving I often think of that phrase, and go stately to wherever I'm off to. I cannot speak Tamil, apart from a handful of words, so we depended on his fairly good English. A lot of the time we drove in a comfortable silence, and I looked out of the window every inch of the way, absorbing the vision of India, fixing it in my heart and mind like a long and wondrous film of everything I saw.

We started the trip from Khader Nawaz Khan Road and left the city via Santhome (St Thomas's) Basilica. Santhome is painted an immaculate bright white and the sky around it always seems dark blue. When I strolled around it in 2002 there was a thriving fishing village on the beach behind the walls. That village was obliterated in the 2004 Christmas tsunami. Now there is a plaque: "In gratitude to God for saving Santhome from the tsunami 2004". The basilica was saved, but not the village, and probably not all the people.

We drove away from Chennai along the straight and sometimes fast coast road. Autorickshaws like buzzing bees competed with thundering lorries. The lorries blasted their horns. Jaunty messages were written on the back. "We Two Have One." "Do Good Have Good." "Horn Please." Brightly coloured, intricate patterns and flowers and peacocks adorned the flat-faced trucks. You could overtake whenever you wanted and it didn't matter which side. Wrecks of buses and lorries were cordoned off by inadequate lines of small stones while the dead or injured waited for someone to attend. An ambulance might shriek by.

The flat landscape along that road was familiar. Palm trees in the distance, then the sea. Pockets of emerald paddy fields with women bent double planting each individual blade. In those days, before they widened the road, there were villages along the edge. Thatched huts in their own small compounds behind thatched walls where children and women walked and bullocks strolled and dogs slept and pigs snuffled around the rubbish. I could smell the rubbish from the car, and the woodsmoke and stagnant water. Often the rivers were dry – just wide stretches of pale, cracked earth that couldn't be used for dwellings. The bridges had white walls. The earth beside the road and in the fields was red and the air was hot and my skin felt warm and sticky. Long stretches of tall Indian trees were ringed in black and white. As a sleepy child I used to watch their endless procession from the back seat of the car. I thought they were painted as a form of road safety but now I think it's to do with protecting the trees from disease.[15]

Intermittently along the roadside, green coconuts were piled high and a solitary seller waited in the heat for a car to stop, for a thirsty passer-by. The seller made a hole with their sharp curved knife

[15] In fact, it may be both: https://timesofindia.indiatimes.com/city/chennai/following-indore-civic-body-paints-trees-to-reduce-accidents/articleshow/91844052.cms

and you drank the fresh juice through a straw. When finished, you returned the nut to be cracked open and the soft flesh scooped up, ready for you to eat. So delicious. Along the road the familiar wayside shrines were still there. We stopped so I could walk among the larger than life-size plaster statues of horses and warriors and gods, all painted in strong colours. And there were darker, more mysterious places where I walked quietly and with care. Clearings with shadowy arrangements of sticks and stones and sacking in dusty shade and the small bowl of milk for the cobra who resided there.

We stopped at the Mahabalipuram Shore Temples, famous for stone carving and where hundreds of small shops line the entrance road to the town. The pavements were crowded with giant gods and other enormous statues and stone festooned the streets. Mahabalipuram is an ancient Pallava dynasty site going back to the seventh century. In the old days, with Mum and Jan and Dad, we walked on the beach to the temples and could touch the stone and look at the carving and there was only us and we were quiet and respectful. Now it is always crowded and the temple is fenced off and you queue to pay to go in. Hundreds of small shops sell shells which they will paint your name on, and plastic gods and things that twirl or glisten and shine, and sugary sweets and crystal-pink candy floss. Swarms of people in deep red robes form bulks of the crowd and gather in large clusters on the seashore. The sea breeze ruffles their red and ochre clothes.

Thyagu and I were aiming for Pondicherry and Sadras was on the way. The ruins of the fort were more overgrown, but the elephant stand and the well and most of the buildings were there and as they had been when we went for our picnics with the Newnses. I walked around the cemetery and over the collapsed walls to the beach where we used to swim. I could see Jan in her swimming costume by the well, having water poured over her and down her front, and I could see her laughing and hear her shrieks from the cold.

In Pondicherry I stayed in a French colonial house with a flat roof outside my bedroom window where I could sit in the mornings and hear the birds and the traffic prepare for another day. And I could hear the sound of sweeping in a nearby courtyard, the soft shush-shush of the stalks of the moving broom.

From Pondi we drove to Kodai, with a night in Trichi[16] on the way. The hills the hills the beloved hills. The drive and views and feel of the chilling air were deeply familiar. The smell of the trees and the woodsmoke and cows and the sound of water

---
16 Tiruchirappalli.

and bells. I went to Lisieux Cottage and through the chocolate gate, up to and around the school. A nun took me through the buildings; the school now provided courses in accountancy and IT and the financial support for local girls and young women to attend. I went to Flis Gibson's house. I walked for miles up quiet roads and those now busy with traffic. I saw houses with names I knew where I had played in the garden. Many were now gated shut and left empty and a few years later some modern building would be there. I went to Spencer's which smelt the same and still did delicious cakes. The lake still had its lilies and scrawny ponies still trotted round it and the streams were there and some of the falls we knew. The drenching of memories was so intense and so very vivid that my heart sometimes physically hurt. I felt I was in a twilight world, neither in the past nor the present but fully connected to both.

I descended from the clouds of Kodai and returned to the plains, the plains, the beloved plains of Chennai, via Cuddalore.

Staying in Cuddalore

On my way to Kodai, while staying in Pondicherry, I spent a day with Thyagu looking for a house I had been to in a place called Cuddalore, not too far from Pondi. I had stayed there with Mum and Dad in 1966 and I had vague memories of it. Dad and I had gone out in a small boat and I had caught a fish which we ate that evening; there was half a mouthful each. It was known as the Parry's Bungalow as it was built and owned by that company, and it was built on the ruins of Fort St David.

We set off through unchanged rural India. We drove past flat earth and paddy fields, slow-paced carts pulled by bullocks, and children and women walking, tending herds of goats. Washing lay on the roadside and piles of rice were being threshed and sieved. Tall palms – some solitary, some in perfect rows in gorgeous groves – were silhouetted on the landscape. The village houses had thatched roofs and mud walls painted green, bright turquoise, pale peppermint, ochre or maybe discoloured white. A solitary family buffalo stood sleepily tethered nearby. We passed Hindu shrines and burial places with crosses. We passed stalls and small shops and music which blared and then faded. A noisy political rally. A village puja. A small wedding. Cows meandered and tried to munch the goodness from rubbish and cardboard. Dogs slept or suddenly crossed the road. Chickens strutted with children and pigs got in the way.

We stopped and asked and eventually, a long way down a small and rarely used road, we finally found the house. A caretaker-housekeeper was there with two of his helpers. They were happy to show me around once I told them the story of staying there with my family and how I had caught a fish. The house was immaculately kept and was gorgeous. Solid, large, probably 1940s, with verandas and a beautiful garden. The view was of green leafiness, across a tranquil backwater to a sandbar in the distance and then on out to sea. I stood and gazed and physically felt the tranquillity. I decided the spirits of my ghosts were with me on this trip.

Anandin was the main housekeeper and he told me that with permission it would be possible for me to stay a few nights in the house. I would have to go to the Parry's company premises just outside Cuddalore. We arrived at the enormous factory buildings and were allowed through the gates. I was escorted to an office near the front entrance where I explained my wish to an efficient but rather bemused-looking man. He asked me to write precisely what I wanted on a piece of paper. I did so as carefully and clearly as I could muster, as if it were for an exam. The paper was taken to the managing director – and not long after, so was I.

Mr Mathiyalagan and Mr Veeramani could not have been more wonderfully warm or kinder. I showed them the 1966/7 diary and they photocopied the pages about our stay in the bungalow. They gave me tea and said they would check with Head Office in Chennai and let me know the next day. I was then taken by car to an enormous house, which they called a bungalow, on a leafy Parry compound, where I was told I could 'freshen up' and where a delicious full-blown lunch appeared from nowhere. I couldn't believe the hospitality, all based on my whim to ask if I could stay in their company guest house. I felt I needed to clarify the financial situation as I imagined it could cost several arms and legs. I tried to carefully word the fact that if it were very expensive I may not be able to stay.

"Oh no," they said, "you don't pay for memories. You would be our guest."

I was ready to go straight back to Pondi after that but Thyagu thought I should go to Chidambaram Temple. Shoeless and in the heat for several hours, I was glad to get back to my room and ponder the happenings of the day.

While in Kodai I heard from Mr Veeramani from Parry's that I could stay at the Fort St David bungalow on my way back to Chennai. I probably could have made it as long as I liked, but we agreed the two nights, which fitted well with my return to stay at the Madras Club.

On my first evening in Cuddalore I sat on the downstairs veranda and wrote my journal while my supper was being prepared. The veranda was semicircular with pillars supporting the upstairs veranda of the same shape onto which the bedrooms opened. Pots of plants skirted the shallow steps which went down to the lawn, and a low white wall, part of the original fort, marked the edge of the garden. Thick greenery sloped down to what seemed to be a river but was actually a quiet backwater of the sea. The lamps from the house threw weak light onto the garden, beyond which was pure darkness. I could hear crickets, the breeze, chirps of night birds and lulled voices from inside the house. It was truly, truly peaceful. I sat in that gorgeous place, my supper being cooked, my bedroom and bathroom immaculate and ready, sipping a cold beer and feeling totally looked after. The meal was fresh fish, dhal, vegetables and chapatis. Really, what more could a person want?

In the morning I woke up early and sat on the upstairs veranda which my bedroom opened on to. I think there were two other bedrooms, but no one else was staying. The sea was just over a sandbar a few hundred feet away and directly onto the house was the backwater, calm and quiet. Birds were waking up and tuning up and silent fishing boats glided by. Other boats, with motors, chugged in that nice slow way that simple old motor boats chug. Being so early, I also inadvertently saw the morning 'proceedings' of a number of local men squatting in the waters nearby.

I sat on the verandas, I walked around the garden and along the road to the endless Coromandel beach. A man from Parry's took me to the original East India Company building where there are vast rooms of gigantic ledgers all filled with meticulous writing. The history carefully maintained. I read books about the company and about Thomas Parry and saw the church where he is buried with his ten-year-old son who died on the same day, 14th August 1824.

I had papaya for breakfast, and freshly squeezed orange juice, and chicken curry with lots of other tasty bits for lunch. My washing was done and ironed. I was relaxed and peaceful and utterly content. If someone had said I could live there – I would have.

In the evening I ate another lovely supper. Anandin watched me eat every mouthful and helped me to more if he thought I was running out. Thyagu came in and stood beside Anandin and I told them what a beautiful day I'd had. Anandin remembered his father and himself at nineteen when I was at the house with Mum and Dad. He told me he had two sons and two daughters, "all married". Then Thyagu said, "The problem, the real problem" – and I knew he meant the sadness – "is that you have no daughter to come here and read your diary, to know what you see now, and to follow you." He looked sad when he said it, as though he understood. I wanted to break down but instead I managed to smile. I told him he would have to remember me if he came to Cuddalore in the future. He said when he came to Cuddalore in the future he would always think of me and my mum and the diary. I think he will, which is a lovely, rather heart-wrenching, thought.

Room 2

From Cuddalore I returned to Chennai where I stayed at the Madras Club in Room 2. I felt a bit lost and solitary on my first evening, not knowing where exactly I should or could go to eat or drink or sit. But I had a drink in the bar and then a chicken sizzler; sizzlers seemed very popular on the menu, along with other Western delights such as shepherd's pie and caramel custard.

Groups of people sat in the bar or the dining room and seemed very at ease with each other and at home in their surroundings. They spoke in English with very occasional Tamil or Hindi words. The women especially were beautifully dressed and I felt I could do with far better clothes and some jewellery.

The rules of the Club and the dress code are really quite exacting. The time of day and the area of the Club all matter and men in particular need to watch their step. Sandals may be worn until 8.30 a.m. on the veranda, but not after this hour, and not in the River Room or Cupola Room or any of the other rooms in the Club, but may be worn in the library.

There is a grid with nineteen items of clothing listed and ten different areas of the Club, and some are divided into time zones – until 8.30 a.m., between 8.30 a.m. and 8.30 p.m., and after 8.30 p.m. The clothes range from bush shirts with side cuts of all styles to pyjamas / kurthas [17]/ rubber slippers. It is easier for women, who mainly have to be dressed 'with decorum'. And there are different rules for children of different ages in different parts of the Club.

In the morning, breakfast was at small tables on the wide veranda overlooking the lawn. The trees and shrubs were thicker now so I couldn't see the river. Crows crowed and small rose-ringed parrots tumbled in and out of the trees making an enormous racket. Occasionally a plane flew overhead. The Club is on the flight path for certain flights and over the years we have got to know the 11.15 Lufthansa or the early-morning BA back to Heathrow. Strangely, the sound isn't wrenching or roaring but oddly distant and quite reassuring, and it accentuates the peace rather than disturbs it. I had fresh papaya and

---
17   A loose shirt or tunic.

butter-jam-toast and also a masala dosa. The toast tastes slightly salty but the south Indian coffee is good and that veranda is still my favourite venue for breakfast in all the world.

Mr Subbiah was chairman of all the Murugappa Group and knew my dad from his work and friendship with older members of the family. It was Subbu who had given the OK for me to stay at the Fort St David bungalow. He invited me to dinner at his home with his wife and other members of his family and Mr Mutiah, who has written several books on Madras. Subbu thought I might like to visit TI Cycles at Ambattur, where Dad was based and where he worked for so many years. He arranged for a car to pick me up early the following day and take me for a tour of the works. They were producing 130 models of bicycles and 10,000 bikes a day. I was shown around and had things explained in a simple and interesting way. I was shown what used to be Dad's office, and the boardroom, which had a photo of Dad on the wall.

We went by car to the company training centre, passing a school, a college and a hospital all built and run by the Murugappa Group. I was presented with a bunch of flowers and a large board at the entrance said 'Welcome' to me by name. Along the walkways and in the dining room were large framed photos with details written beneath. There were lots of 'Mr BA Forsyth, at the inauguration of…' or 'with Sir…' or 'with the Minister of…' – Dad, smiling out of the photos, looking spruce in his crisp white shirts and bowties, involved in his task of sharing the company's achievement. I realised it was 18th February, the anniversary of his death fifteen years before, and there I was in the country he loved at the place he loved to work, looking at photos of him which still hung in honour of previous achievements. I didn't dare mention the date as I couldn't trust myself not to get tearful.

After the training centre, I was taken to another factory which he set up, the Diamond Chain factory. The words were familiar from childhood as he probably talked about it to Mum on the veranda at Khader Nawaz Khan Road. There was another 'Welcome' sign and I was given a basket of roses and a short presentation about the development of the factory, starting with the time of Dad. I had done my best with my limited wardrobe but very much wished I looked more like the Queen. Finally I was taken back to Chennai, to head office, which is Tiam House at Parry's Corner. From the seventh floor I looked at the view of the harbour which Mum wrote about in the diary of 1966/7.

Back in Room 2, I pondered the happenings of

the day. The amazing courtesy and generosity and remembering of times past. What a legacy for Dad – forty years later he and his work were still valued. He would have been pleased by my day.

I had been away for just under three weeks and had covered a lot of ground. Apart from retracing steps and indulging nostalgia, I also visited new places, like Kanchipuram, where I bought a silk sari at vast cost which is still all folded in its box. I went to areas of Chennai that I had probably been to but didn't remember; they would have anyway changed beyond recognition. I went to the Mylapore area with its shops selling silver and gold and stalls with bright glass bangles. There is a small, manageable temple there with an approachable elephant and gaggles of temple priests, unusually young and laughing. I discovered Fab India with its handloom cotton clothes and homewares, and Nali Silks with its acres of glistening colours strewn across counters which seem to go on for miles. I met and got to know the Davieses, who had known my parents. They now lived in Singapore but spent two months at the Club every winter. I met Mr Mutiah, who included some of my old photos in the book he was working on, and I reconnected with Subbu. There was not a moment of time that I would have changed. I saw and did everything I wanted and more.

Thyagu picked me up to take me to the airport. He arrived early and said he would like me to meet his family. I was ready to go, so thought it a lovely idea. I met his grandma and grandad and other family members. They put a faded pink plastic chair in the middle of the room and they all stood around me and smiled. I was offered sweets and water. I was anxious about the water but took a small sip and nibbled the very sweet sweets. Such a tricky position, not wanting to cause offence but also not wanting stomach trouble with a very long journey ahead. My childhood bouts of dysentery haven't set me in good stead.

Back to Yorkshire

T had phoned me several times a week while I was on the trip. He got up in the small hours of the morning to let the dogs out, which coincided with my early morning wake-up and so was a good time for a call. He was interested and lovely to talk to. We weren't 'together' but in this way we were the best of friends. On my return he sat through hours of videos. I still do think it extraordinary and really, deeply sad that so much good can become so utterly smothered. So wasted. Sometimes you find, years later, once the smoke has gone and all is calm, that the good is still there and hasn't been completely extinguished.

But at that time our death throes were lengthy and painful. It just seemed to go on and on. It had started long before the trip to Chennai and continued when I got back. We lived in the extremes of good and bad and in ordinary life we erred on the side of the awful.

Months passed. I mainly just worked and felt lonely and constantly fatigued. He watched television in his house and I watched television in mine and sometimes we relented and watched it together, which was never a good idea. I ate too much and put on weight. I sat on a chair in front of the tele with a mountain of profiteroles on my lap and a glass of vino beside me. I couldn't believe the sight of myself in the mirror. How did that happen? How could that be me?

Work was exhausting and seemed pointless. There was always more than you could do, but it had to be done, and very thoroughly. I came home smelling of prison — a stale, bitter smell of bodies and breath with an over-note of the toast that the officers cooked through the day. And I dwelt on the people in there, some with histories which anyone would struggle to survive. Young ones rattled through detox, and men of all ages self-harmed.

More months passed and I was afraid that T and I would live out these death throes for ever. I couldn't picture any other rest of my life. I couldn't see how this would have an ending. I made the decision that if I were still in the same situation this time next year, I would have to top myself. That decision truly cheered me — it gave me a sense of control, a firm plan B and the impetus to start the process of making real changes in myself. Someone said, "You are responsible for your own happiness." I just kept repeating that phrase.

I hadn't seen T for several months but spent Christmas '02 with him and his mum, Olwen. That would be our last full day together and the last time I would see Olwen. I think of her often. When I see someone with a similar walk, vigorous but bent with her arms held out behind her. Her cheekiness and laughter. I picture her jiving with Mum or stroking the dogs or trying to make T see sense. She called him Teh, in the Welsh way. I know her death a few years later nearly tore him apart.

India, 2003

Yet again, I am amazed at the wonders of human resilience. Even tiny choices can help us make mammoth change. Packed and optimistic and in reasonable shape, I set off for Chennai again. This time my intention was to not only look back but also look forward, even though I wasn't sure what to.

I touched down on 2nd March 2003 at about 1.00 a.m. and went straight to the Club, where I had arranged to stay, in Room 2. Despite the late hour the Club required me to fill in at least three lengthy forms with multiple carbon copies. Entries were made in cloth bound books the size and weight of a table. A few weak lights attached to the outside walls lit my walk from the office to my room. The river smelt high and the air was muggy and mosquitoes were out in millions. March, instead of last year's February, made a big difference to the heat, even at 4.00 a.m.

The next morning Thyagu appeared, as arranged. During my first few days we set out to complete my plans of places I wanted to see – Little Mount and St Thomas' Mount and the church of Our Lady of Expectations, the immaculately kept British War Cemetery, the Gandhi Memorial and Guindy Park. The park was shady with pinky-yellow earth and lots of ants which reminded me of the park I used to go to with Ayah. It was supposed to contain various animals, like a zoo. There was a dusty path with signs pointing off it saying 'Otter' or 'Wild Something', but half the containers were empty and those that weren't were not a good sight to see. Small round huts with thatched roofs and railings so you could see in; inside, a solitary, striped, foxy-looking animal walked to and fro in misery, smelling sky-high and looking slightly deranged. The snake house in the park is famous but I couldn't face going in. I was puce and drenched with the heat.

I went to an area called T Nagar. People, bullocks, autorickshaws, bicycles, buses, cars, and scores of children and dogs vied with each other for the meagre space on the roads. Beggars had their chosen pitch outside shops or at junctions where cars had to stop. They had empty eyes and absent limbs and the women carried babies on their hips. They reached through open car windows or raised their palm to your face. They touched their mouths in a gesture of needing food. Women with expensive shopping walked past; some gave a few rupees. There were hundreds and hundreds of small stalls and shops on the main and side roads, almost all selling silk and cotton. I was on a mission to match some fabric for Deepa, who I worked with in Armley Prison. I thought it would be an easy task, but no. The temperature was almost unbearable and I was bright red and shiny and my hair went in several directions, sticking up or out or down with sweat.

Moving around in that intense heat had made me really unwell by the time I was back in Room 2. I was shivering and aching and my skin hurt, like the first bad stages of real flu, with the added bonus of sharp stomach pains and needing the loo every few minutes. I knew I needed to drink water to counteract the dehydration, but it just went straight through me till I was literally running clear. At one point I took my pillow into the bathroom to save me going back and forth to bed. Oddly, maybe stupidly, I wasn't worried. I knew it was heatstroke and that it would eventually pass. The dehydration probably was rather risky, but luckily that didn't panic me at the time.

By lunchtime the following day I felt able to try a fresh lime soda, with salt instead of sugar. I sat in the shade on the wide veranda, under a fan. I was still aching but felt a lot better, and at least the soda stayed put.

In the afternoon I gingerly walked to the Boat Club down the road and in the evening I went to the bar for another fresh lime soda and to risk something simple to eat. People sat in groups, chatting and laughing together. I sat, contented, on my own. I have never minded being alone in public places, in restaurants or bars. I know many people, especially women, feel conspicuous and uncomfortable but for some reason, luckily, I don't. I just enjoy or get on with whatever I am there for. I might read or write but usually I'm happy to think my thoughts and observe the other people. I spoke to a couple of British men, one of whom had approached me. I felt they were just being sociable as I was on my own. I went off to my room early to catch up on the sleep I had missed the night before. Unfortunately that wasn't to be; I spent another night in the bathroom.

The following morning one of the men from the previous night phoned to see if I'd like to go to a restaurant with him that evening. I thought it a little bit swift, but anyway the answer was obviously no. I explained about my stomach. A short time later I was cautiously sipping yet another fresh lime on the veranda when the man, Patrick, turned up –

complete with rehydration powders and Imodium. He seemed very sure and reassuring, so I took the lot. He phoned again in the early evening to see how I was and I agreed to go to dinner. That was our first 'date'. Patrick still loves that story.

I met up with people and visited places on my own, including a trip to Kodai, but while I was in Chennai I spent a lot of time with Patrick. He was a persistent pursuer with calls and flowers and wanting to take me away. At one point I was worried he might turn out to be a stalker or someone with plans to sneak anthrax into my luggage. Anthrax scares had been prominent at that time. He looked different from people I had previously known, more grown up and older, and his non-social-worker-y background meant he thought very differently too. I learnt and understood things about him within the first few weeks. He was dogged, he made quick decisions and sometimes, socially, he could miss the beat. He had a son and a daughter who he loved to talk about, and he nursed (and still nurses) his guilt for having caused such massive change in their lives. He had been in Chennai for several years, working for a well-known company. He had taken early retirement and had since worked freelance on projects to help a close friend. That friend had died on the night of my arrival and had been buried on the 3rd. Patrick said

Robert had left him but brought him me instead.

In many ways we seemed an unlikely match but there were things we had in common. We shared a quiet wonderment about what we saw and did not feel a need to discuss it. We were both unattached with no one to hurt if we chose to be together – we had both been married and would not forget the pain our separations had caused. We both felt our lives would be happier if shared, rather than being lived alone.

We walked around his local area. Hot, busy streets with lethal, uneven pavements and small shops where he was known and people waved hello. I met the barber where he had been going for years despite his dearth of hair. We went on drives outside the city to quiet places where we just walked and looked. And I had the synaesthesia sensation, as I so often do in India, when my senses blend and my edges soften and I hear the heat and smell the sounds and feel the light on my skin. The rural roads were pale and dusty and lined with trees, and the trees had many branches. The leaves were sparse and shade was wide but thin. Babies wrapped in cloth bundles hung from the branches while their mothers worked in paddy fields nearby. They looked like ripe fruit, ready to pick, large and round and heavy. We walked by a river full of pelicans. We ate giant prawns by the sea. I met a couple he knew who held a small gathering one evening so I could be introduced. Over the years we saw them often and they became my friends. Anneliese had lived in Chennai for decades; she knew Doctor Somesekar and his wife.

In the evening we went to Elliot's Beach. I had been there many times as a child, but only in the day. Miles wide and long, at the end of each day it becomes another world — a cool-down place where all of Chennai goes. There is a noisy road full of traffic, where you hope to park, and then the beach and shallows and in the far distance tankers are moored with empty ocean beyond. People gather in their hundreds to meet and eat and talk and feel the breeze at the end of a scorching day. Women are dressed according to their custom, maybe salwar kameez or saris or skirts with blouses and veils. Fabric flutters, it is airy and bright and light. Children play on simple, homemade, hand-cranked roundabouts, and men in robes ride ponies along the shore. Separate voices rise above the chatter as sellers declare their wares. They ring their bells and repeatedly shout as they push their cart along. Tea, candyfloss, kites and other coloured things on strings. Patchy music blares but gets lost in the air as you pass it, and bright plastic chairs are arranged in rows in front of food stalls where tasty treats sizzle and give off gorgeous smells. Dogs sleep in narrow shade. Their closed eyes look so sweet. Couples sit on the sand, they lean in together and take selfies on their phones. Whole families and clusters of women stand fully dressed, up to their knees in sea. Saris gleam, they are soaking wet and the colours have become even stronger. And then the sky turns grey and pink and turquoise and silhouettes of birds fly by. The twilight is quick and soon it is fully dark and strings of small lights are turned on. I love Elliot's Beach in the evenings.

In the early hours of the morning, Patrick waved me off at the airport. A friend of his was a manager there so he arranged for me to be whisked through ahead of the lengthy queues. We are still in touch with that friend and see him when we visit Chennai. Lionel is tall and elegant, dignity personified. He sends me Anglo-Indian recipes and relevant snippets of history or news by mail. He wants to preserve what is left of his dwindling culture.

Each time I leave India, I am never sure that I will see it again. That is OK. Each visit feels complete. But this time I did hope I would see Patrick again. He had been good for me and to me. Our timing was eerily right. He was leaving India for good in just a few weeks and while I was there he was already half packed and starting to say his farewells. He had bought a house to return to, in Plymouth, where he was from. I was baffled by how someone so different from my previous choices could feel so inevitably right. Perhaps the place where we met gave strength to romantic notions. Perhaps my ghosts had conspired to make our paths converge.

Finally

A few weeks after my return to England, I met Patrick at Heathrow and he came straight up to Yorkshire. For the next few months he spent a lot of time with me, but also made trips back to Plymouth so he could see his daughter and settle into his house. His son lived in Japan. I was still working in the prison but within three months I had given in my notice and put my house up for sale with a view to moving to Plymouth. Life was too short to be spent going up and down motorways. I still had Jan's flat in Surbiton as well as the Yorkshire house, so I wasn't putting any of my eggs in anyone else's basket.

I immediately looked for work in Devon and within a few weeks of moving I started my new job. It seemed extraordinary and rare that there were no obstacles for us to overcome. No distant geography to contend with, complicated finances to tie up or painful loose ends of relationships which had to be resolved. The move was a risk but one I knew was worth taking, and thank goodness I did.

Patrick and I have been together now for nearly twenty-three years. I didn't know there could be such consistent caring for such a long period of time, and an absolute absence of ever wishing to cause me hurt or harm. We have been back to India many times, the last being January 2024. We base ourselves in Chennai but travel around a lot, and I have been to new places like Cochin and Mysore, Lucknow and Varanasi, Kanyikumari on the southernmost tip, and all around Rajasthan. Patrick and I travel together beautifully. We see sights in similar ways, and now we have our shared memories of India as well as our separate ones. We have also travelled to other places, some of which I went to on my 1985 trip – Hong Kong and Japan and Thailand – and also new ones like Taiwan and Cambodia and Vietnam.

Over the years, since leaving Yorkshire, I have worked in mental health, at a hospice and in general social work. No money for social care, of course, then as now, which is why the NHS is in a mess. Astonishing how governments just can't understand that simple and obvious equation. I liked those jobs but not as much as probation – the unsung backbone of the criminal justice system. Despite the exhaustion and the never enough hours in the day, I loved the depth, the interest and the meticulous nature of that work. I chose not to go back into it, although I was offered a temporary post when I first arrived in Plymouth. I knew it would be too all-consuming. I retired several years ago and am still amazed and relieved on a Sunday night that I needn't wonder with dread what unexpected crisis awaits me on the Monday morning. Patrick did some part-time work and then he retired when we moved from Plymouth to Cornwall.

Through work I met new people, a few of whom have now become real friends. I see and speak to them often. We meet in favourite places or they come here or we go to them in Plymouth or Totnes or Torquay. Patrick comes from a large family so has siblings and in-laws around, and we see them from time to time. I like them. They were welcoming to me from the start.

Since a very young age I have had an affinity with slightly muddled-up souls, with people prone to prodding at life, perhaps just a fraction unhinged. There are fewer around me these days. I do sometimes miss them, but I value the ones I know.

I see and talk to Lynne who lives with her husband, Neil, in London. Her life is full of family and interests and work which helps other people. Her art is on our walls. She has a son called Leo, and when he was very little she asked if I would be his legal guardian if anything happened to her. I felt that was such an honour. He is grown up now and is due to be married soon.

I'm also in touch with people from Milan days, like lovely Lizzie, and we see Norman and Aldo in Rome. They always look after us beautifully when we're there. Norman texts news and views and snippets that make us laugh. I speak to our old family friend, Mary Mac, on the phone. She is housebound, so we visit her in London when we can. She is now one of very few people on earth to have seen my family house, with us in it, on Khader Nawaz Khan Road and in Kodai. She knows Ayah. We can speak about Jan. And I love to hear her talk about her family who my mum and dad knew so well. We see Gill and Steve in France or here and Gill and I have very long chats on the phone. I cannot think of an emotional nook or cranny we haven't explored at some point.

I have friends with whom I feel a level of acceptance and familiarity which is comforting beyond words. A mutual respect and will to understand each other's choices, including some of the odd ones – most of us have made some of those. We know each other's contexts. There is nothing we need to explain.

My cousin Bren now lives in Devon and we

are in frequent touch. We can talk about present happenings as well as family and childhood. I miss her mum, my special Aunty Peggy, Dad's sister. Bren's two grown-up children have three children each. I think of them all as 'family' and feel lucky and happy to have involvement in their lives.

I have other cousins, two of whom I rarely see but am in touch with from time to time. Joan, who lives in Derbyshire with her husband Paul, and Molly Anne, who was named after my mum, are the daughters of one of Mum's brothers. I feel connected to Joan and Molly with some of their thinking and taste. They are very much Newburys, as Mum was.

Simon is remarried, with no children, and lives in San Francisco with his wife. Over the years we've exchanged infrequent mails — one from him when David Bowie died as we had been Ziggy fans and knew all Bowie's words, and more recently he told me about an accident he'd had. Injuries and shock and what feels like a future in jeopardy can tend to make you look back. We share many memories of ourselves as very young, of our families and our travels and Milan. D is still there, I think. There have been sporadic requests for friendship which I have chosen not to pursue. In the early days, many many years ago, he occasionally sent a message and I would occasionally phone. He answered without surprise as if expecting my call, at that actual minute. He said we are always connected.

T was in Ireland but is back in Yorkshire now. He contacted me via Facebook not very long ago. Initially I found it unsettling – as Lynne would say, it stirred up the muddy pond. He says he has found real peace now, although still has a lot going on. He has written two books, about his present and his childhood. I think we will stay in touch.

Knowing that another person in this world – someone I may no longer see – contains and values and can recall the exact same memory as me, is an extraordinary sensation. Old memories from my previous life, before I arrived where I am. It verifies my past existence and makes me feel not alone. I am predisposed to a sense of disconnect which in some ways I have grown used to. Perhaps it stems from the volume of moves I've made and the quite early separations. But it's reassuring to exist in someone else's mind. Old stories we both remember, some of life's major happenings, or just things that make us smile.

There is also a layer of closeness with people who have known my family, who knew who they were and liked them. I was so lucky with the workings of mine, the ease I felt and how I loved being with them. I miss them. Sometimes I still think I can pick up the phone to Jan. Not everyone has the luck of an easy family. I have sat in the tension of some, a silent twilight zone of disapproval and disappointment. Easy to displease. They have their reasons, I know.

Patrick's daughter, Nat, and her partner, Paul, live not far away so we see her and her beautiful little girl, Martha, fairly often. Nat loves beaches and skies and her beloved black Sprocker, Reg. She is good at thoughtful gestures and Martha calls me Nanny. I feel very lucky to have that title having bypassed being a mum. On Mother's Day this year Nat sent me a card saying 'Bonus Mum'. A lovely and happy thought which I very much hope to live up to. Patrick's son, Ben, lives in Hokkaido with his Taiwanese wife, Sherry, and their two little girls, Izzy and Millie. The girls are fluent in three languages – Japanese, Mandarin and English. They are all settled in Japan. They work hard and seem to have made a good life there. They live in a beautiful landscape which is often covered in deep snow and they send video clips of themselves snowboarding, even their three-year-old. We have visited them in Japan and Taiwan but in recent years they have come here to see all the family. It's a long journey, so we are grateful to them for doing it instead of us.

Sometimes, just briefly, I feel some perverse nostalgia for the extremes of the life I knew, the stretched-taut tension and rawness, the drinking too much and dancing, the battle of wits and the crying with laughter and the hanging on by a thread. Sometimes I think I may have become a damped-down version of myself, blurry-edged and a bit too blended-in. My wit, in both senses of the word, may have blunted. Perhaps that is age, the absence of work, or just my efforts to not rock the boat I am in. A circumstantial loss. I can't have things all ways.

We are lucky, with the people we have around us and where we live – in beautiful countryside, just minutes away from the sea. I look out from the upstairs of buses, which we love to use, or the top of our steep garden, which Patrick tends with great care. Water, woods, pastures and hills everywhere. Animals graze and sometimes we see herds of deer. I can hardly believe that this is where I live. With Patrick, supremo whistler, a definite do-er, a happy soul - and the best looker-afterer I've known.

Life is generally easy and most of the time it is as tranquil as I would want. There are also intermittent crises. Us or people close to us, in the midst of life events. Illness, death, relationships, complicated family goings-on. That old tapestry, which keeps us on our toes.

I do need things to keep me on my toes. Adventures and journeys and some useful work that I really ought to do. I'm not quite where I want to be when the music stops, and I don't mean geographically. That is a work in progress, which this writing is now part of.

It is over a year since we last went to India. Soon Patrick will start whistling the BA tune again – the one they play before take-off and landing. BA is the only airline that flies direct to Chennai from Heathrow. With his repeated whistling he plants in my head the sensation of being there and the idea of going again. The next thing I know I am looking at seat plans on planes and checking the cost of tickets. I'm phoning the Club to ask about Room 8. Room 8 is the one we like now. It is at the top of the very same steps I ran down to see Ayah when I was thirteen years old. But strangely, I don't feel an absolute need to physically return to India. I know it exists, and it's where I feel happy and at home. India is my parallel universe, and I can go there any time in my head.

www.ingramcontent.com/pod-product-compliance
Lightning Source LLC
Chambersburg PA
CBHW020412080526
44584CB00014B/1294